TCM TURNER CLASSIC MOVIES

FALLING IN LOVE AT THE MOVIES

ESTHER ZUCKERMAN

ROM-COMS
from the
Screwball Era
to Today

RUNNING PRESS
PHILADELPHIA

Running Press
Hachette Book Group
1290 Avenue of the Americas, New York, NY 10104
www.runningpress.com
@Running_Press

First Edition: December 2024

Published by Running Press, an imprint of Hachette Book Group, Inc. The Running Press name and logo are trademarks of Hachette Book Group, Inc.

The Hachette Speakers Bureau provides a wide range of authors for speaking events. To find out more, go to www.hachettespeakersbureau.com or email HachetteSpeakers@hbgusa.com.

Running Press books may be purchased in bulk for business, educational, or promotional use. For more information, please contact your local bookseller or the Hachette Book Group Special Markets Department at Special.Markets@hbgusa.com.

The publisher is not responsible for websites (or their content) that are not owned by the publisher.

Print book cover and interior design by Susan Van Horn
All images courtesy of Turner Classic Movies

Library of Congress Cataloging-in-Publication Data has been applied for.

ISBNs: 978-0-7624-8446-1 (hardcover); 978-0-7624-8447-8 (ebook)

Printed in China

1010

10 9 8 7 6 5 4 3 2 1

To Bob

CONTENTS

INTRODUCTION

I CAN'T REMEMBER THE FIRST ROM-COM I FELL IN LOVE WITH, but I know that loving rom-coms is an intrinsic part of my general obsession with movies—an obsession that I've now made a profession. I do remember, however, seeing *You've Got Mail* for the first time. I was eight years old, and my family had a tradition of going to the movies on Christmas Eve. It was 1998 and we picked the latest from Nora Ephron—apparently so did the rest of the Upper West Side. It made sense: The movie is both Ephron's exploration of then-new technology of email and ode to the neighborhood where she (and most of my family) lived. When we got there, the theater on 68th Street had oversold the screening. In the hazy memory of childhood, I recall people plopping down in the aisle to watch Meg Ryan and Tom Hanks banter and bicker before ultimately realizing they are meant to be together. Eventually, the ushers sent the overflow into another screening room.

I've watched that movie countless times since then, so much so that it's hard to recall details of the first time I viewed it beyond that excited environment. But I remember the *feeling* of watching it with a crowd of people seeking the satisfaction only a good romantic comedy can provide.

What is that sensation?

OPPOSITE: Cary Grant and Rosalind Russell in *His Girl Friday* (1940).

It's similar to what I felt when I saw *Notting Hill* (1999) in a theater in Los Angeles's San Fernando Valley. I became so infatuated with the story of a British bookseller played by Hugh Grant who meets a movie star—Julia Roberts, naturally—and falls in love, that I named a Barbie doll Anna Scott, after Roberts's character.

It's the feeling I got watching *Roman Holiday* (1953) on repeat and determining that Gregory Peck must have been an amazing kisser because of the way he embraces Audrey Hepburn. Or when I decided to make sure I'd seen all the collaborations between Katharine Hepburn and Cary Grant because I couldn't get enough of their spark. I fell in love with the rom-com before I understood romantic love myself. I became enchanted with the way my gut dropped during those crucial moments when the music swells and the faces get closer, the kiss incoming. I always knew these movies were slightly unrealistic, but that heightened sense of the absurd only drew me closer. These were the film equivalents of tucking into a perfect meal, the kind that left me satiated but not stuffed. They were like settling into cool sheets on a hot night. They were the epitome of comfort even when they were just a little bit sad. And that's why I gravitated to them year after year.

In high school, I dressed up like Annie Hall, the eponymous character from Woody Allen's 1977 movie, for Halloween. In a haze of Anglophilia, I rewatched *Four Weddings and a Funeral* (1994) over and over again, identifying more with Kristin Scott Thomas's sardonic best friend than with Andie MacDowell's pretty American interloper, all while loving Hugh Grant's self-deprecating hero the entire time. I felt like I saw myself in James L. Brooks's *Broadcast News* (1987), relating deeply to Holly Hunter's perpetually stressed-out, know-it-all news producer, caught between two men and her career.

In later years, when the rom-com's box-office success faded, I rejoiced whenever I got a new film to treasure. I could feel that familiar heart-swelling excitement when Jenny Slate and Jake Lacy danced on a couch to Paul Simon in *Obvious Child* (2014) and when Henry Golding hustled through a crowded airplane to Constance Wu as Coldplay's "Yellow" in Mandarin blared in *Crazy Rich Asians* (2018).

Even as my taste in cinema evolved, I have always returned to rom-coms. They are what I want to watch when I need something that I know will make me happy.

What *is* the cinematic romantic comedy? Bluntly: It's a love story where the obstacles to love are humorous rather than tragic, for the most part. Writing about the comedies of the 1930s and 1940s, the philosopher Stanley Cavell called them comedies of "remarriage," arguing that the genre is "an inheritor of the preoccupations and discoveries of the Shakespearean romantic comedy." Most of the movies Cavell writes about can be deemed "screwball comedies," the zany style that emerged in the Great Depression. These are fast-moving and delirious in style. In the foreword to Ed Sikov's book *Screwball: Hollywood's Madcap Romantic Comedies*, the critic Molly Haskell writes that "these fables of love masquerading as hostility were largely an elitist variant of the eternal battle of the sexes."

Gendered conflicts are inherent to a lot of rom-coms—from *The Lady Eve* (1941) to *Tootsie* (1982)—but not all of them, as the rom-com has grown and changed with the eras, introducing queer couples and people who don't conform to a strict binary that was once the standard in society. At the same time, through all these evolutions of the genre, there often exists the question of whether two seemingly incompatible people can realize they are perfect for each other.

Within this structure there are subgenres. There are workplace rom-coms (*Broadcast News*, for instance). There are fantastical rom-coms (1988's *Big* or 2004's *13 Going on 30*). There are raunchy rom-coms, like *Knocked Up* (2007). While their branding has shifted over the years, romantic comedies have been around since what is essentially the beginning of cinema, weathering the Hays Code, the rules instituted in 1934 to maintain morality in Hollywood. And while the circumstances through which the lovers find each other may change, there are elemental similarities that have survived and evolved all the way from Shakespeare's *Twelfth Night* in 1602 to *Maid in Manhattan* in 2002.

When the rom-com exploded in the late 1980s through the early 2000s, the formula of the genre started to solidify, a process that led to much affectionate mocking. (See, for instance, the rom-com as 2014 rom-com parody *They Came Together*, where Paul Rudd and Amy Poehler bond over their mutual love of the intentionally vague "fiction books.") Yes, rom-coms often rely on familiar beats: the meet-cute, the second-act breakup, the mad dash toward the happy ending. And yet to reduce rom-coms to their tropes is to underestimate the magnificent breadth of the genre. It's easy to think of rom-coms as just one thing: Meg Ryan and Tom Hanks *or* Julia Roberts and Richard Gere *or* Kate Hudson and Matthew McConaughey. But the rom-com has been around essentially since the invention of cinema. And those latter modern-day classics took cues from everything that came before, whether explicitly—without Ernst Lubitsch there would never have been a *You've Got Mail*—or through inheriting their stylistic flourishes.

Why do we love rom-coms? Rom-coms, generally, offer the promise of the Hollywood dream. For the most part, at the end of each movie, the couple gets together and presumably lives happily ever after. You largely get what you came for when you watch a rom-com: pithy dialogue, kissing, an uplifting experience.

I say *largely* to add an important caveat. Because, of course, that's not always the case. In the vast history of cinematic rom-coms, creators have played with the formula, throwing obstacles in their characters' paths. But even when things don't turn out perfectly for the lovers, rest assured that you might experience that hit of endorphins from watching a couple lock eyes across a room, feel those butterflies in your gut when they share an exchange.

As Alice Wu, who wrote and directed the landmark and under-rated queer rom-com *Saving Face* (2005), told me in an interview: Rom-coms are an act of wish fulfillment for both the audience and the creators. They often imagine a world where finding love can happen in the space of ninety minutes. Even if the couple has to part by the time the credits role, there's some hope there.

The rom-com genre is not perfect. It's fallen on hard times, propagated ridiculous expectations, and been branded as cheesy and regressive. But it's also wonderful and often fascinating in a way for which it doesn't often get credit. With this book I want to celebrate but also

Tom Hanks and Meg Ryan bicker at Zabar's in Nora Ephron's *You've Got Mail* (1998).

elevate the rom-com and give it the serious consideration it deserves. That doesn't mean giving it a pass for some of its failures—the occasional sexism, despite ostensibly being a genre aimed at women, for example—but while these movies are easy to pigeonhole as just "comfort viewing," they are also not the goofy, smooth-brained, easy entertainment that their reputation might imply.

If you're looking for a soup-to-nuts history of the rom-com, this is not it. It's more of a *selective* history. It's by no means comprehensive, but it gives an overview of how rom-coms have shaped and been shaped by the world around them. So, are you ready to fall in love?

PERFECT ROM-COM MOMENT
WHEN HARRY MET SALLY . . . (1989)

Which perfect moment do you choose in a movie entirely composed of perfect moments? It's hard, for sure, but there's no question that for all of *When Harry Met Sally . . .*'s incredible scenes, Harry's New Year's Eve speech takes the cake.

There have been plenty of rom-com finales where one party runs like mad to declare his or her love, but perhaps none match the heart-stopping sweetness of Harry's confession to Sally. It's New Year's Eve and he has realized the grim mistake he has made in letting their friendship lapse following a one-night stand. So he jogs through the streets of New York and lands at the party where he knows she's going to be.

The countdown is imminent, and she is mad that he's there. But, finally, as the ball prepares to drop, he lets loose: "I love that you get cold when it's seventy-one degrees out. I love that it takes you an hour and a half to order a sandwich. I love that you get a little crinkle above your nose when you're looking at me like I'm nuts. I love that after I spend the day with you, I can still smell your perfume on my clothes. And I love that you are the last person I want to talk to before I go to sleep at night. And it's not because I'm lonely, and it's not because it's New Year's Eve. I came here tonight because when you realize you want to spend the rest of your life with somebody, you want the rest of your life to start as soon as possible."

In that moment Harry says to Sally everything she and we want to hear. He loves her because of who she is—quirks and flaws included—and we love them together. And it all happens when her hair is perfectly curled and the tinsel of the holiday is all around them. It's a dream.

WHO MAKES ROM-COMS? AND HOW DO THEY DO IT?

ASK ANY CASUAL FILM FAN TO NAME A ROM-COM DIRECTOR, you'll likely get one answer: Nora Ephron. Sure, there are other names that might get tossed out. Nancy Meyers possibly. Richard Curtis maybe. Garry Marshall perhaps. But it often always comes back to Nora.

Nora Ephron is to rom-coms what Martin Scorsese is to gangster movies. But that is a reductive comparison. Neither Nora nor Marty is just one thing, and it's true that most filmmakers don't really make only one type of film. Scorsese, for instance, has indeed made some of the most indelible mob movies of all time, but he has also made a period romance (1993's *The Age of Innocence*) and a children's film (2011's *Hugo*). Before writing 1989's *When Harry Met Sally . . .*

Ernst Lubitsch with Margaret Sullavan and a portrait of himself on the set of *The Shop Around the Corner* (1940).

Ephron co-wrote *Silkwood* (1983) for Mike Nichols, a harrowing true-life drama about a factory whistleblower. In 1990, just after the release of the rom-com that all future rom-coms would emulate, she even wrote a gangster comedy, *My Blue Heaven*, noted for its relationship in subject matter to Scorsese's *Goodfellas* (1990). It's hard to pin down any creator as just one thing.

It's even harder to do so when discussing rom-coms from the Golden Age of Hollywood, between the invention of talkies in 1927 and the radical transformation of the industry in the 1960s. William Wyler, who made the quintessential romantic comedy *Roman Holiday* (1953), also made the legendary historical epic *Ben-Hur* (1959). Billy Wilder could direct something as delightful as *Sabrina* (1954), about a chauffeur's daughter and the wealthy men who employ her father, and something as acidic as *Ace in the Hole* (1951), where Kirk Douglas plays a muckraking journalist who relies on human suffering to get a story. Howard Hawks directed the zippy likes of *Bringing Up Baby* (1938) and *His Girl Friday* (1940), but also helmed the noir *The Big Sleep* (1946) and the western *Rio Bravo* (1959). Frank Capra was responsible for *It Happened One Night* (1934), maybe *the* defining screwball rom-com, and the classic Christmas weepy everyone knows and loves, *It's a Wonderful Life* (1946).

Nora Ephron on the set of one of her rom-com masterpieces, *Sleepless in Seattle* (1993).

Harold Lloyd and Jobyna Ralston in *Girl Shy* (1924).

And yet all these directors belong on the Mount Rushmore of rom-com auteurs, along with Nora and Nancy and their ilk, and we can trace a brief history of the genre through the people whose art shaped it.

Where does the rom-com begin? There's Shakespeare, of course, whose plots have been filtered throughout time, reworked again and again. But, for our purposes, I'm interested in the cinematic rom-com, which itself has been part of the fabric of the medium since its inception. It's easy to forget that the rom-com existed before the invention of talking films, with the luminaries of the silent world making movies that fit the description. For instance, 1924's *Girl Shy*, starring Harold Lloyd, is a rom-com about a young man who is petrified of interacting with women in real life but writes a book about his suave ways with the opposite sex called *The Secret of Making Love*. When he meets an actual girl on a train and saves her dog, he must put his fantasies into practice. Buster Keaton too had the rom-com in his arsenal with

Claudette Colbert and Clark Gable negotiate their sleeping arrangements in *It Happened One Night* (1934).

films like 1924's *Sherlock Jr.*, a comedy about the fantasy of being a romantic hero, in which Keaton's projectionist dreams that he's a detective in a movie and gets to save the girl. And, before he transitioned to sound, Ernst Lubitsch was making silent rom-coms like *The Marriage Circle* (1924), about intrigue and infidelity among a group of married couples in Vienna. In that film, the Museum of Modern Art once claimed, Lubitsch "discovered the genre that he would elevate to the heights of formal perfection and emotional resonance: the sophisticated romantic comedy."

But what's also true is that the rom-com as we know it in the twenty-first century is most indebted to the "screwball comedy," defined by wacky circumstances, sexy scenarios, and light satire. The screwballs emerged in the 1930s, a time of shift for Hollywood, beyond even the addition of dialogue. As Ed Sikov writes in *Screwball*, the growth of the screwball coincided with the implementation of Hollywood's pro-duction code aimed at sexual or otherwise immoral content, known as the Hays Code. "Talented directors, writers, and stars were cer-tainly not about to get rid of sexuality, so they simply found ways to slip it in on the sly," Sikov explains. There were many Pre-Code rom-coms, but, according to Sikov, the imposition of morality restrictions sparked inspiration even as it offered challenges.

The term *screwball* was first used in 1936 to refer to Carole Lom-bard's performance in *My Man Godfrey*, but the movie that (perhaps unfairly) gets the most credit as the inventor of the genre in its purest form is *It Happened One Night*. The comedy, directed by Frank Capra, paired the stars Claudette Colbert and Clark Gable as Ellie Andrews, a rich girl running away from her family to elope, and Peter Warne, a newspaper reporter who offers to help her if she gives him the exclusive. Despite their initial hostility toward each other, the mutual attraction almost becomes too much to bear as their trip goes on. The curtain they put up in their shared motel room for privacy inevitably drops in the sexy final beat.

The list of genius screwball directors is long and includes the pre-viously mentioned Hawks, as well as Leo McCarey (1937's *The Awful Truth*) and Mitchell Leisen (1939's *Midnight* and 1937's *Easy Living*). But in this broadly defined era, you can point to two filmmakers who, like Nancy and Nora, are easily synonymous with this world: Ernst Lubitsch and Preston Sturges.

Nora Ephron and Nancy Meyers are often spoken of in the same breath. And it makes sense. In a world where lauded female directors are still rare, they both became iconic for movies that merit countless rewatch-ing, the kind of flicks that make you stop and settle into your couch no matter what your other plans. But while their respective oeuvres could be described as "cozy," they also represent the possibilities within the rom-com genre. You cannot mistake a Nora Ephron movie for a Nancy

Meyers movie. Nora's movies are steeped in a New York style of chatty intellectualism. They are like attending a wonderful dinner party, filled with the smartest people you know. Nancy offers up more of a California brunch—whether set in the Hamptons or Los Angeles. They are breezy. Her movies are like mimosas. Nora's are like martinis. These differences are similar to the gap between Lubitsch and Sturges—they also had distinct flavors from each other.

Lubitsch was a German immigrant whose films had a sort of jewel-box quality to them. He became known for what was called the "Lubitsch touch," phrasing that highlighted his knack for capturing subtle gestures and elegant situations. Preston Sturges, on the other hand, was more outwardly ribald. He lived a transient life growing up, which he documented in his posthumously published memoir. His mother was a quasi-socialite always in need of a buck and he didn't know his father. He would eventually take the surname of his stepfather, a stockbroker from Chicago named Solomon Sturges. An unsettled existence jetting between France—where his mother was best friends with the famed dancer Isadora Duncan—and Chicago is evident in his films, where money and romance tend to collide in hilarious fashion. He gleaned chaotic characters from his own chaotic life and put them in his films.

On a surface level, it's easy to see the influence Lubitsch had on Ephron given that she remade his classic *The Shop Around the Corner* (1940), transforming it into *You've Got Mail* (1998). But for my purposes Nora is more Preston to Nancy's Ernst. Nancy, like Ernst, relishes art direction, the sparkling spaces that her characters occupy; Nora's movies thrive because of their dialogue. In a Daily Beast article, Nora once recommended Sturges's *The Palm Beach Story* (1942), specifically highlighting a zany scene at the top of the action where Claudette Colbert's heroine meets a rich old man who hilariously diagnoses her problems. "I tell everyone I know who wants to be a screenwriter to watch the scene at the beginning of the movie," she wrote, adding, "It's a lesson in specificity."

The ménage à trois of Ernst Lubitsch's *Design for Living* (1933).

Lubitsch's films have a dainty quality, which isn't to say his works aren't deceptively sexy. Take, for instance, *Design for Living*, made in 1933 before the imposition of the Code, in which an advertising artist (Miriam Hopkins) meets two struggling creatives, a playwright (Fredric March) and a painter (Gary Cooper), on a train ride to Paris. They form a fast friendship and all start cohabitating, which gets considerably messy, since both artists are in love with her. She switches partners midway through, and by the end of the movie they are all giggling together, falling into a dogpile.

Like *Design for Living*, many of Lubitsch's works were set in Europe, even if biographer Scott Eyman contended that his movies "take place neither in Europe nor America but in Lubitschland, a place of metaphor, benign grace, rueful wisdom." *The Shop Around the Corner*, arguably his work with the longest tail, is set in a Hungarian leather goods store. It's a saga of warring employees who are secretly pen pals, ultimately becoming the inspiration for Ephron's *You've Got Mail*. A German Jew, Lubitsch was working in Hollywood as Hitler was rising in his home country. And while he made what is maybe one of the definitive skewerings of the Nazis in *To Be or Not to Be* (1942), about a Polish theater troupe trying to outwit the SS, he also gave America pretty portraits of the continent at a time of war and genocide.

Eyman was not a fan of the phrase "Lubitsch touch." He called it "as insultingly superficial a sobriquet as that of calling Hitchcock 'The

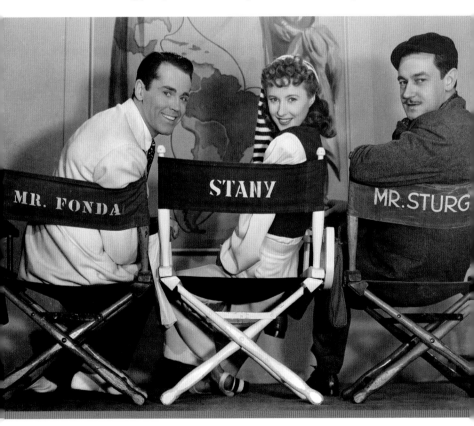

Henry Fonda, Barbara Stanwyck, and Preston Sturges on the set of *The Lady Eve* (1941).

Master of Suspense.'" According to Eyman, Lubitsch had a "tradition of insinuation, of a delicate but intoxicating, self-conscious style." Still, it remains an apt shorthand for the almost magical quality Lubitsch conveys. His movies are like tiny bells ringing; they chime in a graceful way, like what you might hear when you enter a shop.

Sturges, on the other hand, comes in like a marching band. His most famous romantic comedy, *The Lady Eve* (1941), casts Barbara Stanwyck as stunning con artist Jean Harrington, working her angles on a luxury cruise liner. She sets her sights on Charles "Hopsie" Pike (Henry Fonda), a wealthy amateur herpetologist, whom she seduces and lures into her card game gambit with the help of her partner (Charles Coburn), posing as her father. When he eventually realizes what's going on, he is enraged and never wants to see her again. She, however, has fallen in love with him, and later, back on land, decides to make him pay for his rejection by posing as the eponymous "Lady Eve." She arrives at his fancy home barely disguising herself save for a ridiculous accent. An easy mark, Pike falls for this cultured woman from abroad, somehow oblivious to the fact that it's the same fast-talking gal he initially rejected. They get married only for "The Lady Eve" to reveal that she has a sordid past, scandalizing Charles. This Eve scares him right back into the arms of his original lover, whom he doesn't realize is the same woman. There, he haplessly confesses that he's already married. She says she is too. Kissing ensues.

In his memoir, Sturges writes that *The Lady Eve* was inspired by his experience running into a woman with whom he was besotted three years earlier. In his account, she wasn't all that special. "I realized that it isn't so much that love is blind," he explained. "It is that love is bewitching." He added, "This proved an extremely useful insight when I made a little picture called *The Lady Eve*, in which Henry Fonda fails to recognize Barbara Stanwyck, not because she disguised herself in any way, but because the Lady Eve couldn't hold a candle to the girl in his memory, the girl on the boat." Sturges didn't name

"The Lady Eve" after his onetime romantic interest, however. That was an homage to a "ladyfriend" named "the Lady Eve Waddington-Greeley." According to Sturges, "She didn't hang around very long, but years later I called a picture *The Lady Eve* in souvenir of her."

Sturges loved exploring the folly of the rich and the desperation of those who need—or covet—money. *Sullivan's Travels* (1941) followed a wealthy movie director (Joel McCrea) who wants to do good by depicting America as it is, a journey that leads him to realize that what people really crave is entertainment. In *The Palm Beach Story* (1942) Claudette Colbert and McCrea play a financially down-on-their-luck married couple. They are still attracted to one another, but she decides that she is a burden to him because of her inability to help provide, so she plans to get a divorce and marry a rich man who can help them all out. Unlike the more genteel farces of Lubitsch, Sturges is rawer, bawdier, and more concerned with class.

I feel that same energy watching Nora Ephron movies, despite the reputation she has for soft entertainment, the kind of movies the whole family can enjoy. Her movies can be warm and fuzzy, yes, the kind of entertainment that elicits mood boards with supposed "fall fashion inspo." But that is selling her short. Remember: *When Harry Met Sally . . .* is rated R.

That 1989 movie, written by Ephron and directed by Rob Reiner, linked Ephron's name forever with rom-coms and marks a turning point for the genre, the moment that ushered in a heyday of the form that coincided with big box-office returns. Still, Ephron was always more complicated than that legacy would suggest. Like Sturges, Ephron was persistently observational, turning the details of her life (and her friends' lives) into cinematic material. Her motto was "Everything is copy." She idolized Dorothy Parker, the member of the Algonquin Round Table most known for her quippy takedowns.

Ephron started in movies when she cowrote the screenplay for *Silkwood* with Alice Arlen. She then adapted her novel *Heartburn* into a 1986 film for director Mike Nichols. The book is a lightly fiction-alized account of the time her ex-husband, Carl Bernstein, cheated on her when she was pregnant with their child. It's funny and very bitter, less a story about love than a story about what happens when love goes awry. Though *Heartburn* was not a runaway success as a movie—even Nora admitted it was a "flop" when it opened—Ephron dived into the world of screenwriting.

But then came *When Harry Met Sally . . .*, the movie that would forever cement Ephron's reputation as the queen of the rom-com. The idea for the movie started with a pitch from Rob Reiner, who would go on to direct the film. Reiner had a slightly different idea in mind, but after a heated conversation about gender stereotypes, Ephron came up

Meg Ryan in the climactic scene of *Sleepless in Seattle* (1993).

with a new concept: What if she explored the question, in movie form, of whether heterosexual men and women can really just be friends? As her test subjects, she created Harry Burns (Billy Crystal) and Sally Albright (Meg Ryan). They meet just after college on a road trip where they bicker the entire way and then keep running into each other until they eventually become pals and then fall in love.

When Harry Met Sally . . . is both savvy and a huge crowd-pleaser. Though its message is ultimately that, no, men and women cannot be friends—or at least these two cannot—it gives equal weight to men's and women's perspectives, a result of Ephron treating her research the same way she did her journalism, interviewing Reiner and Crystal about their experiences to fuse them with her own.

With When Harry Met Sally . . . Ephron had found her niche. She went on to direct Sleepless in Seattle (1993), pairing Tom Hanks and Meg Ryan in a love story that, by mere description, should sound like a horror setup. In Sleepless, Hanks is Sam Baldwin, a widower in, yes, Seattle, whose young son calls a radio show and tells the world that his dad needs a new girlfriend. The sad, sweet story catches the ears of listeners around the country, including Ryan's journalist Annie Reed, who starts pursuing a story about him, but finds herself smitten. In other hands this would be the saga of a crazed stalker—and, sure, to some people it still is—but Ephron's ability to romanticize the idea of a persona makes it endearing. The outlandishness of the plot is a throwback to the movies that Ephron adored, ones that she makes constant reference to throughout her own films. Sleepless in Seattle steals its climax at the Empire State Building from An Affair to Remember (1957), which the Sleepless characters reference on-screen. (Most famously, Rita Wilson sobs while recounting the plot.) And then in You've Got Mail, Ephron went ahead and remade Lubitsch's The Shop Around the Corner for the nascent era of the internet, where the would-be lovers, again Hanks and Ryan, exchange missives over AOL rather than on paper.

Diane Keaton and Jack Nicholson offer romance for adults in *Something's Gotta Give* (2003).

Meyers in many ways had a parallel career. Like Ephron, she began screenwriting before directing, teaming with her (now-ex) husband Charles Shyer on screenplays like *Private Benjamin* (1980) and *Baby Boom* (1987), both third-wave feminist classics about women figuring out whether they can have it all. Shyer directed the latter, but Meyers would come to usurp him in style once she started directing her own movies. Though it wasn't her directorial debut that truly established her rom-com brand. Young Lindsay Lohan in 1998's *The Parent Trap* was adorable, certainly, and Meyers paid special attention to the attraction between the parents, played by Dennis Quaid and Natasha Richardson. But once Meyers made 2003's *Something's Gotta Give*, she created her own ethos. Take mature stars—forget your

William Holden, Audrey Hepburn, and Billy Wilder on the set of *Sabrina* (1954).

ingenues—put them in linen and a gorgeous kitchen and let sparks fly. Almost more than her romantic pairings—which have included Jack Nicholson and Diane Keaton in *Something's*, Meryl Streep and Steve Martin and Alec Baldwin in *It's Complicated* (2009), and Cameron Diaz and Jude Law in *The Holiday* (2006)—Meyers became known for making romances about aspirational lifestyles.

Meyers has made her love of Lubitsch explicit with a project she deemed *Paris Paramount*, a nod to a quote from Lubitsch: "I've been to Paris, France, and I've been to Paris, Paramount, and frankly, I prefer Paris, Paramount." Meyers wrote in her 2022 announcement of this venture, "It's from a quote by the brilliant and elegant comedy director (dare I say creator of the romantic comedy) Ernst Lubitsch. The movie is about a group of people making a film and the magic and mystery of what we do. As always, Lubitsch said it best." As of publication it's not yet known whether this project will come to fruition, but one thing is certain: It's a handshake from one aesthete to another.

If Lubitsch had a direct successor that would be Billy Wilder. Along with collaborator Charles Brackett, Wilder wrote some of Lubitsch's classics, including *Ninotchka* (1939) and *Bluebeard's Eighth Wife* (1938). When he moved into directing himself, he more than proved he was a master of any form. Until the end of his life, there remained a sign in his office that read, "How would Lubitsch do it?"

Wilder's triumphs include *Sunset Boulevard* (1950), a Hollywood gothic classic where fading beauty turns deadly, and the slinky noir *Double Indemnity* (1944). But he also thrived making movies that specifically followed the path laid out by Lubitsch and Sturges. One of his greatest is 1954's *Sabrina*, which stars Audrey Hepburn as the daughter of a chauffeur for a rich family, hopelessly in love with David Larrabee (William Holden), the playboy son of her dad's boss. In the opening sequence of the film, distraught with rejection, she tries to

Jack Lemmon and Billy Wilder.

kill herself, only to be rescued by Linus Larrabee, the older, stiffer son portrayed by Humphrey Bogart. Sabrina goes off to Paris to attend cooking school, where she becomes cultured but remains fixated on David. When she returns home, stylish and refined, David finally takes notice, only he's engaged to another woman, a more socially appropriate match. In trying to keep David away from Sabrina, Linus decides to woo her. What is initially a ruse is transformed when real emotions take hold.

A rom-com that begins with a suicide attempt sounds pretty dark, and, indeed, Wilder's films often had deep wells of melancholy. One of his other masterpieces, *The Apartment* (1960), is an even darker exploration of romance blooming between broken souls. Midway through the movie Shirley MacLaine's Fran Kubelik, an elevator operator having an affair with a married man, also tries to kill herself.

The iconic final moment of *The Apartment* (1960).

She's found unconscious in the apartment of CC "Bud" Baxter (Jack Lemmon), the man who has been pining after her (and renting out his home to the bigwigs at his office for their clandestine meetups).

The Apartment ended up winning the Academy Award for Best Picture and received heaps upon heaps of praise. In a note found in Wilder's personal papers at the Academy Museum of Arts and Science's Margaret Herrick Library, the novelist George Sumner Albee wrote to Wilder: "I seek out Wilder pictures as if I were gleaning an ash-heap for emeralds, but, even so, I must write to say that for sheer faultless directorial skill applied to the material in hand THE APARTMENT is one of the half-dozen all-time greats."

Wilder had a knack for delivering great performances from actors. With *The Apartment* and *Some Like It Hot* (1959), Jack Lemmon did among the finest work of his career. In *Some Like It Hot* and *The Seven Year Itch* (1955), Wilder helped create some of Marilyn Monroe's most iconic screen moments.

The influence Wilder had on younger filmmakers can best be summed up in the way someone like Cameron Crowe idolized him. Late into Wilder's life, he sat for a series of interviews with Crowe, who, like Wilder and Ephron, was a journalist turned filmmaker. In them, Crowe had Wilder walk through his entire career with him. Crowe wanted to emulate Wilder, so he made him share his secrets. He engineered a passing of the torch with approval from Wilder himself, who liked Crowe's *Jerry Maguire* (1996). "Billy Wilder respected me, I think, to a point before he saw *Jerry Maguire*, but after *Jerry Maguire* he took me seriously," Crowe once said. (Crowe had, in fact, tried to get Wilder to cameo in the movie.)

Crowe's career is particularly indicative of how you can trace the lineage of rom-coms from generation to generation. Yes, he was obsessed with Wilder and you can see that in his oeuvre, with his melancholy romances and deeply flawed figures, but he was mentored by another god of the rom-com world: James L. Brooks.

Brooks came from the world of television. He cocreated classic sitcoms like *The Mary Tyler Moore Show*, *Rhoda*, and *Taxi* before turning to film. His first directorial effort, *Terms of Endearment* (1983), is remembered as a tearjerker, but his follow-up *Broadcast News* (1987) fell squarely in the realm of romantic comedy, even if Brooks didn't initially think so. *Broadcast News* transfers the spirit of Howard Hawks's preeminent journalism rom-com, *His Girl Friday*, to the world of television. On one hand, it's a movie about the rise of infotainment and blurring the line between celebrity and newscaster. On the other, it's a love triangle between three incredibly driven people: a beautiful anchor who is not all that smart (William Hurt), a neurotic reporter (Albert Brooks), and a highly competent producer (Holly Hunter). The movie, yes, invests you in the idea of who Hunter's character will end up with, but it does so by forcing you to reckon with a changing news industry that values looks and celebrity over information.

As James L. Brooks's career went on, he kept working in this space, making movies that melded romantic-comedy tropes with ambitious concepts. He tried (and ultimately struggled) with *I'll Do Anything* (1994), a Hollywood satire that was first shot as a musical and eventually released with its songs removed. However, he was successful yet again with 1997's *As Good As It Gets*, which starred Jack Nicholson as a crotchety romance writer with obsessive-compulsive disorder who becomes entangled with the waitress, played by Helen Hunt, at the diner he frequents. It won Oscars for both Nicholson and Hunt.

In a 2004 interview, Brooks shared his theory on romantic comedy, saying: "I love romantic comedy, I really do, but I think you have to have another idea that you're chasing along with romantic comedy so I begin to have an idea I'm chasing." Those feelings are evident in his works, which always feel like they are pushing the genre beyond its confines. His movies are long and sometimes unwieldy, trying to place love stories alongside other big ideas.

But Brooks's legacy also lies in the careers he helped facilitate. He was a producer on Penny Marshall's *Big* (1988) and Wes Anderson's debut *Bottle Rocket* (1996), as well as Kelly Fremon Craig's teen movie *The Edge of Seventeen* (2016) and her Judy Blume adaptation *Are You There God? It's Me, Margaret* (2023).

With Crowe, however, he found his most simpatico acolyte. Starting with 1989's *Say Anything*, Crowe established himself as the defining creator of Gen X rom-coms. His movies often had classic "boy chases girl" scenarios, but they also aimed for sweeping emotions and big, generational statements. *Say Anything* gave us John Cusack holding up his boom box to Ione Skye's window as Peter Gabriel plays. Crowe's 1992 follow-up, *Singles*, canonized the Seattle grunge scene, and 1996's sports-agent romance *Jerry Maguire* established "You had me at hello." And it all goes back to Billy Wilder.

PERFECT ROM-COM MOMENT
SABRINA (1954)

It's supposed to be a clandestine meeting with the man she's had a crush on for decades. In Billy Wilder's 1954 film *Sabrina*, the title character (played by Audrey Hepburn) returns from a sojourn in Paris a new, more sophisticated woman, and her longtime unrequited love, David Larrabee (William Holden), one of her chauffeur dad's employers, has finally taken notice of her. They arrange to meet up during one of the Larrabees' lavish parties on an abandoned tennis court. But there's a problem: David is engaged and his family—especially his brother, Linus Larrabee (Humphrey Bogart)—doesn't approve. Linus foils David's plans—David's strategy of putting champagne flutes in his back pocket yields a bum full of crushed glass—and goes in his stead.

A toast on the tennis court for Humphrey Bogart and Audrey Hepburn in *Sabrina* (1954).

Hepburn is standing in the darkened space in perhaps the most stunning of the Givenchy gowns she wears with its white and black embroidery, her face framed by the moonlight. Sabrina is still smitten with David and aware that Linus might have ulterior motives, but her canny diagnosis of the situation turns into a flirtation. It seems to catch Linus off guard. She's smarter than he gave her credit for, and by the time they are slowly swaying to "Isn't It Romantic?" in each other's arms, there's genuine affection creeping into his posture. She mentions that she, long ago, saw David dancing to the song with another woman in the very same spot. He brings her in close.

"It's all in the family," he says. Her gaze begins to soften too. She's feeling the start of something she wasn't expecting.

You really can't talk about any rom-com post-1977 without discussing the tricky subject of Woody Allen. The controversies that have long dogged Allen's personal life must be acknowledged in the same breath as his work and influence. And yet his work and influence are also impossible to ignore. Allen arguably changed the notion of what a rom-com could be, inspiring many others to follow him.

Even with this complicated backdrop, *Annie Hall* (1977) still reigns as one of the preeminent rom-coms of its (or any) era. The Oscar winner follows the love story between Alvy Singer (Allen) and the eponymous Annie Hall (Diane Keaton). In *Annie Hall*, Allen annihilates the format of a typical romantic comedy, with asides to the camera that break the fourth wall and an ending that is painfully realistic. What if a man who is skeptical about the entire endeavor of love is trapped

Diane Keaton wearing her famous getup in *Annie Hall* (1977).

in his own love story, both infatuated with the woman in his saga and doubtful that it will ever work out? It doesn't, and that's the point—the journey of this romance is still intoxicating. With *Annie Hall*, Allen both subverted rom-com tropes and redefined them. *When Harry Met Sally . . .* directly references *Annie Hall* with Sally's wardrobe of vests and floppy hats and its cutaways to elderly couples talking about their relationship. In fact, the movie was initially perceived as a direct imitation of Allen.

But Allen was not a scholar of the Preston Sturges school of screwballs. In fact, in a 2011 interview, he said he was "never an enormous fan." Instead, he took much of his inspiration and cues from the Swedish filmmaker Ingmar Bergman, whom he idolized. Allen's love of Bergman and his application of that love in the context of romantic comedy is indicative of the way filmmakers' approach to the genre shifted in the 1960s and '70s.

From a bird's-eye view, there doesn't seem to be much room for rom-coms in the era codified by the book *Easy Riders, Raging Bulls*, which gave rise to directors like Scorsese and Francis Ford Coppola. But that's not entirely true. Hollywood was changing, yes, but sexual mores and ideas of love and romance were also changing. And certain directors were interested in exploring those changes using a semi-traditional romantic-comedy format, even if only to question the ideas surrounding love and romance.

You could almost call this the era of "anti" rom-com directors, artists who played in the general rom-com sandbox but were cynical about love and happy endings. That's not to say that the earlier eras of rom-coms were all that prudish. Even the Rock Hudson and Doris Day comedies of the late 1950s and early 1960s have a layer of sex appeal. But it was a wink rather than explicitly spelled out. As the '60s progressed—and the morality restrictions of the Hays Code fell away—rom-coms could engage more directly with sex and all the confusing ugliness surrounding it.

Mrs. Robinson (Anne Bancroft) and Benjamin (Dustin Hoffman) in bed in *The Graduate* (1967).

During this era there's a trio of rom-coms that I like to call the "weird rom-coms," partially because they are hard to classify precisely *as* rom-coms. These movies are *The Graduate* from 1967, *A New Leaf* from 1971, and *Harold and Maude*, also from 1971. They are all rom-coms in which the subject matter is deliciously transgressive. These aren't movies about two beautiful people falling for each other: They are about murder and infidelity and death.

In *The Graduate*, directed by Mike Nichols, a young man named Benjamin Braddock (Dustin Hoffman) comes home from college to find himself seduced by his parents' friend Mrs. Robinson (Anne Bancroft). A setup with her daughter Elaine (Katharine Ross) initially goes terribly wrong. He takes her to a strip club with the intention of making her dislike him, until he winds up falling for her. The darkness that courses throughout the film undercuts how comically wild it would otherwise seem, as it is capped off by a happy ending that doesn't seem all that happy. Benjamin's race to the chapel to stop Elaine from marrying another man would inspire parodies and imitators, but rarely could anyone else capture the unease Nichols lends to this final sequence.

Nichols would eventually direct a more traditional romantic comedy in 1988 with *Working Girl*, about an assistant from Staten Island (Melanie Griffith) who tries to make it in the corporate world of Manhattan. Along the way she falls in love with a handsome colleague (Harrison Ford), who happens to be in a relationship with her boss, a detail that is only revealed over time. Then, in 1996, Nichols remade the 1978 French comedy *La Cage aux Folles* into *The Birdcage*—with a script written by his onetime comedy partner Elaine May, *the* Elaine May, who made *A New Leaf*.

In what was also her directorial debut, May stars as a botany-obsessed, daffy heiress who is wooed by a formerly rich jerk (Walter Matthau) who plans to murder her and take her cash to revive his own fortune. On one hand, it's a disturbing one-sided romance—she genuinely thinks he's interested in her and he's plotting her death. On the other hand, it's the story of a couple so equally bananas they belong together. Her clueless persistence and survival instincts break down his will to acquire her funds, and they end up together. May actually wanted the film to be more disturbing. She explained in a 2006 conversation with Nichols that, "They took a murder out of it. I wanted to do the first comedy in which somebody got away with murder."

The specter of death hovers over Hal Ashby's *Harold and Maude*, perhaps the oddest of these titles, as well. The movie begins with nineteen-year-old Harold (Bud Cort), a young man obsessed with mortality, staging his suicide. But his disaffected attitude shifts when he meets seventy-nine-year-old Maude (Ruth Gordon), who has the opposite perspective on life, despite nearing the end of hers. The conclu-

Elaine May in costume, directing *A New Leaf* (1971).

sion is a sad one—Maude dies—but of the three films mentioned here, *Harold and Maude* might actually be the sweetest. Despite its gothic qualities, it's a genuinely uplifting story about learning to embrace the time you have.

On the other hand, May's follow-up to *A New Leaf*, *The Heartbreak Kid*, released in 1972 and written by the lauded playwright Neil Simon, drips with acidity. The wonderfully nasty story follows a man named Lenny (Charles Grodin) who marries the hilariously annoying Lila (May's daughter Jeannie Berlin) and then promptly becomes infatuated with a beautiful blonde college student, named Kelly (Cybill Shepherd), while on his honeymoon. Lenny does everything he can to keep Lila stuck in their hotel room while he romances Kelly and

Ruth Gordon and Bud Cort in *Harold and Maude* (1971).

sucks up to her parents, who see right through his ingratiation. Lenny ostensibly gets what he wants: He and Kelly marry at the end. But he is left just as unfulfilled as he always was. Roger Ebert described it as "a movie about the ways we pursue, possess, and consume each other as sad commodities."

When *The Heartbreak Kid* was released, the draw was not just May, but Simon, the Tony Award–winning writer of *The Odd Couple* (1968), whose previous successes included 1967's *Barefoot in the Park*. Most of the rom-coms written by Simon don't hold up as well as *The Heartbreak Kid* does, partially because they just aren't as mean. His most famous works now seem dated, rooted in old ideas of how men and women should act. Take *Barefoot in the Park*, about a married couple (Jane Fonda and Robert Redford at the peak of their respective beauty) who move into a dingy Greenwich Village apartment after a spectacular honeymoon at a hotel. As soon as they take up residence in the problematic abode, their personalities start to clash. He's a traditionalist; she's a free spirit. They both want each other to adapt to their ways and are equally resistant to doing so.

Barefoot in the Park relies on the notion that audiences might somehow be at least lightly scandalized by a woman with as little interest in traditional gender roles as Jane Fonda's character, even if Redford is supposed to be the stick-in-the-mud. By the end she has to acquiesce, caring for her uptight husband, while he has to pretend to have a little fun.

Similarly, *The Goodbye Girl*, the 1977 film that won an Oscar for Richard Dreyfuss, is based on an ostensibly outlandish scenario that feels less so today. In the film, a single mother (Marsha Mason) is dumped by her boyfriend, who rents out his room in their shared apartment to a pretentious actor (Dreyfuss). Despite her horror, the actor squats in the room and they eventually coexist and fall in love. Simon's humor is very much of the late '60s–early '70s, and it makes the movies feel old in a way other, even older, movies do not.

Charles Grodin and Cybill Shepherd in *The Heartbreak Kid* (1972).

The big kiss in *Breakfast at Tiffany's* (1961).

None of the Simon films have aged as unevenly as Blake Edwards's *Breakfast at Tiffany's* from 1961. In many ways the movie still sparkles: Hepburn wasn't author Truman Capote's idea of Holly Golightly—she was a blonde in the novella—but she was iconic nonetheless. That image of her pearled neck, with a long cigarette holder, is a dorm room staple for a reason. Hepburn as Holly is glamour incarnate, even if the character is far more nuanced than she first appears. When you're naive, you want her fashion and her oddball tendencies. It's not until later that you start to understand the depth of her sadness. It's a triumphant performance.

It's easy to see why Paul (George Peppard) is so smitten with this creature, even if it's not so clear to modern audiences why she falls into his arms at the end, relinquishing her hard-won independence for his touch. Still, their rain-soaked reunion in the final moments is so spectacularly grandiose, it's entrancing. But as much as you might get swept up in the romance, you are also perpetually reminded that the film also features Mickey Rooney in offensive yellow-face makeup as Holly's angry landlord. It messes with the entire experience, a difficult relic of times past.

Even with such a legacy, you can't discount Edwards, often an exuberant satirist, who was ahead of his time when it came to gender. In 1982, he made *Victor/Victoria*, a musical rom-com starring his wife, Julie Andrews, about an opera singer who pretends to be a man in drag to become a Paris nightclub sensation.

In the '80s and '90s the rom-com began to take its most recognizable shape, largely thanks to the ascendancy of the likes of Ephron. But there were others who contributed to the model of what it would and could be too. John Patrick Shanley, for instance, likes to think of his movies as "human comedies" rather than rom-coms, but it's difficult to see 1987's *Moonstruck* as anything but a rom-com. Shanley was working as a playwright when he penned his ode to falling for the wrong person. Cher stars as Loretta Castorini, a woman who has written off romance and decides to marry a less than desirable man, Johnny Cammareri (Danny Aiello). Johnny is off to visit his dying mother but has one request for Loretta: Get in touch with his brother Ronny (Nicolas Cage). Ronny, who lost his hand in an accident for which he blames Johnny, has decided to wallow in his misery. He's frustrated with Loretta for settling for a man as doltish as his

Nicolas Cage takes Cher to bed in *Moonstruck* (1987).

brother. She's frustrated with Ronny's impertinence. They end up in bed. *Moonstruck*—directed by Norman Jewison, who also made Doris Day and Rock Hudson's *Send Me No Flowers* (1964)—is big and bold in just how romantic it is. Ronny loves opera and the movie itself is operatic. But, as is often the case with opera, the grim reaper hovers around the action. All of the characters are seeking love to avoid thinking about death.

Garry Marshall, also working at the time, didn't deal in that kind of darkness. Marshall made movies that were exactly what they appeared to be: broad crowd-pleasers with big stars and huge hearts. In *Overboard* (1987), he paired real-life couple Goldie Hawn and Kurt Russell. Hawn plays a rich lady who suffers from amnesia after falling off her yacht; Russell is the rough handyman who tells her she's his wife as payback for treating him poorly. But Marshall's most significant contribution to the rom-com canon came in 1990 with

Pretty Woman. The "hooker with a heart of gold" story (and trope) turned Julia Roberts into a major movie star, uniting her with Richard Gere for the first time, in a coupling that would ultimately become one of the most heralded in modern rom-coms. (They would meet again in Marshall's 1999 film *Runaway Bride*.) She is Vivian, a Hollywood Boulevard streetwalker; he's a businessman, Edward, who finds his guard taken down by this beguiling woman. To get a sense of Marshall's sunny touch, all you need to do is learn what the first draft of the script for *Pretty Woman*—initially titled *3000*—was about. Written originally by J. F. Lawton, *Pretty Woman* was supposed to be a *Wall Street* (1987) successor, about money and power, and with an unhappy ending. Marshall, however, saw it as a "combination of fairy tales," he once told *Vanity Fair*. And a fairy tale it was. *Pretty Woman* ends with Edward arriving in a limo at Vivian's apartment to whisk her away to a happy ending. And, while, sure, there are still hints

Julia Roberts was the ultimate "hooker with a heart of gold" in *Pretty Woman* (1990), a fairy tale of sorts.

Hugh Grant and Martine McCutcheon in the grand finale of *Love Actually* (2003).

of the darkness that once existed, you can easily overlook it for the dreamy ending.

Marshall is a man who loves to live in the land of fairy tales when it comes to rom-coms. He made *The Princess Diaries* movies (2001, 2004), featuring Anne Hathaway as a teenager who learns she's the royal heir to a small European country, falling in love on her way to ascending the throne. Some of the last movies of his career were centered on holidays—sprawling ensemble rom-coms featuring major movie stars looking for romance on occasions like *Valentine's Day* (the first; 2010) or *New Year's Eve* (the second; 2011). These movies with their intersecting storylines don't shy from cliché, but there's a pleasure to them, provided by Marshall's earnestness and the sheer amount of talent involved.

Of course, *Valentine's Day* was a clear effort to capitalize on the success of a film by another master of the rom-com: Richard Curtis. Released in 2010, *Valentine's Day* came seven years after *Love Actually* (2003), the controversial mother of this subgenre. By the time Curtis wrote and directed *Love Actually* he was the reigning king of the British rom-com. *Love Actually* was his big swing.

Curtis said he was attempting with *Love Actually* to make a Robert Altman film like *Nashville* (1975) or *Short Cuts* (1993), but in his own wheelhouse. Perhaps because of its scope, *Love Actually* is unwieldy and often goes for pure sentiment over nuance. But it also captures why Curtis had such a pull in this arena: He loves "love," as he has confirmed over the course of multiple interviews. While other rom-com creators might make their art to explore gender dynamics or unrequited longing, Curtis is a big old sucker for love—and that's why it's so easy to love him in return.

Curtis got his start in the world of British television comedy, writing for Rowan Atkinson's historical BBC TV series *Blackadder* and others. But the script that launched him into rom-com history was 1994's *Four Weddings and a Funeral*, starring a young and charming Hugh Grant as a bachelor who attends the eponymous events with his ragtag group of friends, falling in love with a gorgeous but aloof American (Andie MacDowell) along the way. In Grant, Curtis found the perfect hero for his brand of bumbling British romance. Grant was the bookstore owner who suddenly becomes involved with the most famous woman on the planet (Roberts, of course) in *Notting Hill* (1999), also written by Curtis. He was the cad in *Bridget Jones's Diary* (2001), which Curtis adapted from Helen Fielding's novel. And, to swing back to where we started, he was the prime minister in *Love Actually*. The Curtis touch was taking the sort of manic rhythms of British satire and funneling them through the conventions of the romantic comedy. Americans feel refined and worldly watching his films, and everyone can fall hard for the grand gestures, which often involve Grant confessing his love in some sort of extreme circumstance. (He's in the rain. He's at a press conference. It's Christmas and he's the prime minister showing up at random people's houses.) For viewers outside the UK, the Curtis movies also have the benefit of foreignness providing a distinct sort of escapism.

PERFECT ROM-COM MOMENT
MOONSTRUCK (1987)

An amazing rom-com moment doesn't have to involve one of the main characters. After all, secondary players give *Moonstruck* its name. In the middle of the night Raymond Cappomagi (Louis Guss) gets up to look at the night sky. There's a huge moon, and it reminds him of the moon from when Cosmo (Vincent Gardenia) was young and in love with Raymond's sister Rose (Olympia Dukakis). He sounds silly waxing about Cosmo's moon, and his wife, Rita (Julie Bovasso), tells him to come back to bed. He's in the mood and so is she. They aren't young, they don't have movie star looks, but their chemistry is infectious and spreads through the rest of the movie.

Shortly after the release of *Love Actually*, a movie debuted that heralded another shift in the rom-com ecosystem: *The 40-Year-Old Virgin* (2005). Directed by Judd Apatow, it was a rom-com that leaned more heavily on the *com* than the *rom*. The Apatow era popularized the rom-com of male arrested development. These films moved away from the "chick flick" marketing that was affixed to so many of their peers to highlight the schlubs at the center of their stories. The Apatow movies are deceiving. Once you get past the jams and crude jokes, you uncover a streak of what might be considered conservatism and the message that you have to grow up and learn to be a good partner. These comedies were the last gasp for rom-coms at the modern box office before they were pushed out by blockbusters with swelling budgets. But rom-coms have never gone away, and there are plenty of modern-day rom-com makers who have worked in quieter corners of the film world.

The history of rom-coms and their makers isn't linear or simple. *When Harry Met Sally . . .*, of course, has Ephron's Jewish influence, but it was never explicit about it, only coded as such for those in the know. It's certainly not as explicitly Jewish or as much about assimilation as Joan Micklin Silver's *Crossing Delancey* (1988), about a woman (Amy Irving) whose bubbe on the Lower East Side of New

Seth Rogen is a man-child alongside Katherine Heigl in *Knocked Up* (2007).

Taye Diggs and Nia Long explore their sexual tension in *The Best Man* (1999).

York enlists a matchmaker that sets her up with a pickle vendor (Peter Riegert). And it's true that rom-coms about minority groups are often not included when people look at the larger history of the genre, in spite of the joy and innovation they bring.

The face of the rom-com has throughout time been extremely white, but there were also directors and writers of color who did not get as much credit as Nancy or Nora but made inroads in defining what these movies could be. Malcolm D. Lee, for instance, created a rom-com franchise in *The Best Man* (1999), an ensemble film about a group of Black friends coming together for a wedding and all the drama that ensues. Sanaa Hamri, who came from the world of music videos, made two rom-coms, *Something New* (2006), starring Sanaa Lathan, and *Just Wright* (2010), starring Queen Latifah. Hamri's work was notably focused on the Black female experience, telling stories of women's lives where the men are secondary to the protagonist's development.

The world of independent cinema has recently been more conducive to voices that fall outside the homogenous mainstream as well. I think of Stella Meghie's *The Weekend* (2019) or Raine Allen Miller's *Rye Lane* (2023). It's also been a home for voices that want to experiment with or approach topics on a smaller scale. And yet there is one "indie" rom-com that defines success for all others, having reached to the heights of commercial success and audience adoration.

My Big Fat Greek Wedding (2002) went on to gross over $368 million worldwide and become a genuine sensation. It is the little rom-com that could. It is the highest-grossing romantic comedy of all time and the highest-grossing indie film of all time. Nia Vardalos was a struggling actress and writer when the actress Rita Wilson saw her one-woman show, in which she played Toula, her character in the movie. Wilson loved it so much she recruited her husband, Tom Hanks, and his production company to back the film.

But for every *My Big Fat Greek Wedding* there are maybe four or five smaller indie rom-com gems that never made it to universally beloved status. Or there are directors who never really sought that kind of success—Nicole Holofcener, for instance. Holofcener has made rom-com–adjacent films for almost her entire career. Her debut film, 1996's *Walking and Talking*, starring Catherine Keener and Anne Heche, is about what a lot of rom-coms are about—the desire to find love and stability—but ends up being more about a friendship than a romance. The 2013 release *Enough Said*, which pairs Julia Louis-Dreyfus and James Gandolfini, is more traditional. Louis-Dreyfus plays a woman who embarks on a tentative relationship with Gandolfini, all the while secretly befriending his ex-wife (Catherine Keener), a poet who becomes her massage client. Holofcener's work consistently resists any sort of easy categorization, even if she told me that she should be included here. "I make rom-coms. More or less," she said when I interviewed her for *Vanity Fair* about her marital comedy *You Hurt My Feelings* (2023).

The same could be said of Richard Linklater. Do you even count his *Before* trilogy of movies for these purposes? The first two certainly fit the bill. In *Before Sunrise* (1995), Jesse (Ethan Hawke) and Céline (Julie Delpy) meet cute on a train in Prague and spend a day together just relishing in conversation. They are young and love seems like an incredible idea. But then they separate. By the time *Before Sunset* (2004) comes along, he's a successful writer and married, visiting Paris on a book tour. They reconnect and by the end, yes, there are sparks, but there is also the baggage of age. *Before Midnight* (2013) turns them into a bickering married couple, meditating on wish fulfillment. The movies are funny and often romantic, but are they rom-coms? Maybe. Depends on whom you ask. Me? I'd say *Before Sunrise* is, given how it's filled with the fizz of new love; *Before Sunset* is a more mature take on the genre; and *Before Midnight* is definitely not. It's more of an excoriation of the very concept of a happy ending.

Other writers found themselves more firmly lodged in the genre. In the early 2000s, Jennifer Westfeldt had a tiny cottage industry of rom-coms she wrote and starred in (but, at least at first, did not direct). With *Kissing Jessica Stein* (2002) she plays a New Yorker who answers a lesbian's personal ad and finds herself experimenting with her sexuality. *Ira & Abby* (2006), which found her costarring with Chris Messina, is about a couple who impulsively get married and then need to figure out how to coexist. Westfeldt was never primed to be a box-office draw, but her movies and characters captured an Ephron-esque spirit.

When Alice Wu started writing her 2005 directorial debut *Saving Face* she was still working as a computer scientist and wanted to try penning a movie as a challenge to herself. Her writing class instructor told her she had a good premise: A mother gets pregnant and moves back in with her daughter who is also pursuing a romantic interest. But the teacher also told Wu that she would inevitably have to change it. The characters—members of the Chinese community in Queens, New York—would have to be white and the daughter would have to be straight. Wu stood her ground and *Saving Face* was made as is, a gem that's both a rare queer rom-com and one that's a portrait of the world Wu knows. It took her sixteen years to make her follow-up: *The Half of It* (2020), a coming-of-age rom-com that puts a queer spin on Edmond Rostand's play *Cyrano de Bergerac*, also starring an Asian lead. (*Cyrano* had previously been made into a rom-com in 1987 with Steve Martin in *Roxanne*.)

Saving Face toured film festivals before its theatrical release. Once the rom-com faded from the mainstream, film festivals like Sundance were more likely spots to find satisfying rom-coms—many of which experimented with form. Gillian Robespierre's *Obvious Child* in 2014 was one such breakout—a rom-com couched in the story of a woman getting an abortion. *The Big Sick*, released just a couple of years later in 2017, was a similar success. Kumail Nanjiani and his wife, Emily V. Gordon, wrote their own love story into rom-com format. He's supposed to have an arranged marriage when he falls for her. She ends up having a rare disease that puts her in a coma, forcing him to commit to her care while also standing up to his own parents.

This is all to say that the rom-com is still ripe for reinvention. It's never been just Nancy and Nora and Preston and Ernst, and even their work is richer than it first appears. As times change, so do ideas of what love should be, making the rom-com the perfect vehicle to suffuse with cultural anxiety and subversion. Plus, it makes for good entertainment. Seeing the arc of a relationship, even when it ends in heartbreak, is a chance to live vicariously through other, usually more beautiful, people.

CHAPTER

2

THE MEET-CUTE

IF YOU KNOW ONE THING ABOUT THE ROM-COM, YOU KNOW about the "meet-cute"—the adorably happenstance way in which the two lovers in one of these movies first encounter one another. The meet-cute has been around as long as love stories themselves, but over the years it's evolved from a term used by screenwriters and studio executives into something everyone with a passing interest in rom-coms is aware of.

The culprit? Nancy Meyers's *The Holiday*. In Meyers's Christmas-time house-swap film, Kate Winslet's character Iris, having given her English country cottage to a movie trailer producer (Cameron Diaz), is driving in Los Angeles when she encounters an elderly man (played by the legendary actor Eli Wallach) confused on the road. She stops to get out and help him. When she delivers him to his doorstep, he tells her that this was their "meet-cute." She's puzzled. (She's from England, you see, and not familiar with Hollywood jargon at all.) "It's how two characters meet in a movie," he says. "Say a man and a woman both need something to sleep in and they both go to the same men's pajama department. And the man says to the salesman, 'I just need bottoms.' The woman says, 'I just need a top.' They look at each other, and that's the meet-cute."

OPPOSITE: Cary Grant and Katharine Hepburn in *Bringing Up Baby* (1938).

Gary Cooper (left) and Claudette Colbert (center) meet cute buying pajamas in *Bluebeard's Eighth Wife* (1938).

Wallach's character, it turns out, is a screenwriter who becomes Iris's confidant as she navigates her own romantic entanglement. And the scenario he describes is the one from Ernst Lubitsch's *Bluebeard's Eighth Wife* (1938).

The screwball *Bluebeard's*, which was cowritten by Billy Wilder and Charles Brackett, opens with Gary Cooper's business tycoon Michael Brandon shopping at a store on the French Riviera. Despite being a multimillionaire, he's cheap and only wants a pajama top to sleep in. The salespeople are baffled and refuse to sell him just one part of the set. Then, Claudette Colbert's Nicole arrives. She solves the problem because she only needs pajama bottoms. He's smitten and she's unaffected. Though he wonders if she's on a shopping trip for a lover, he ultimately discovers that she had purchased those pants for her father, a faded French aristocrat who will do anything for a quick buck. The plot goes haywire from there. Michael desperately wants to marry Nicole. Nicole's father wants her to say yes for Michael's money. She's at first resistant, but then submits. Alas, on their wedding day she learns that he's been married seven times before and only goes through with it to make a buck on a prenuptial deal. Their meet-cute is, indeed, very cute.

Since *The Holiday*, it feels like the public popularity of the idea of the meet-cute has almost ruined the meet-cute. When a rom-com takes the very phrase as its title, as it did with the forgotten 2022 vehicle starring Kaley Cuoco and Pete Davidson, there's an argument to be made that it's lost its spark. (In that movie there's a time machine and she's actively trying to engineer the meet-cute.)

Where *did* the term come from anyway? The columnist Jack Smith considered himself one of the foremost researchers of the subject. In a 1983 column in the *Los Angeles Times*, he wrote: "When the definitive history of Hollywood and the movies is written, the 'cute meet' or 'meet cute' may receive only a footnote, but if my research is quoted in that footnote, I will treasure it as my claim to immortality." Well, Jack, this is not the definitive history of Hollywood in its entirety, but your work has stood the test of time. Throughout the column in question, Smith is concerned with whether the official term is "cute meet" or "meet cute." It doesn't really matter, but I appreciate his diligence.

Smith quotes the actor Tommy Vize, who claims the term was invented by the legendary agent Swifty Lazar, which made its way into George Axelrod's play and movie *Will Success Spoil Rock Hunter?* (The movie came out in 1957.) The journalist also cites the screenwriter and novelist Anita Loos, of *Gentlemen Prefer Blondes* (1953), whom some other sources credit with the invention of the verbiage for "meet-cute." Loos said: "A cute meet is when Claudette Colbert is in an elevator and drops her purse and a monkey wrench falls out of it and hits Fred Mac-Murray on the foot." Colbert and MacMurray were an early screwball romance team, though MacMurray is arguably better known for playing the horrible boss in *The Apartment* and the man taken for a ride in *Double Indemnity* before going on to sitcom stardom.

Beyond Loos's description, what defines a "meet-cute"? As far as I see it, the partners can't know each other already, and there must be an element of somewhat absurdist coincidence. A hint of serendipity if you will; a dash of happenstance. (And, yes, one happens in the 2001 movie titled *Serendipity*. Kate Beckinsale and John Cusack are both glove shopping.) It's not necessary for a rom-com to have a meet-cute. For instance, I would argue that *When Harry Met Sally . . .* does not have a meet-cute. Harry and Sally have prearranged to drive from Chicago to New York together. Their meeting isn't cute; it's planned. Now, you could argue that when they encounter each other later in the story in the Upper West Side's Shakespeare & Co. bookstore and her friend Marie (Carrie Fisher) tells her, "Someone is staring at you in Personal Growth," *that's* a meet-cute. But it's not their first encounter. The meet-cute is secondary.

The purest meet-cutes are the ones that thrive on improbability, and it helps if they have a hefty dose of sexual spark.

In Howard Hawks's *Bringing Up Baby*, Cary Grant's paleontologist David Huxley first encounters Katharine Hepburn's heiress Susan Vance on the golf course. She steals his ball and he is unperturbed by it. They encounter each other yet again at a fancy restaurant. He slips on an olive she was trying to pop in her mouth. She gets him accused of thievery and then he accidentally rips the back off her dress, forcing him to walk behind her to save her modesty. It's meet-cute after meet-cute after meet-cute, the aggravation ultimately yielding chemistry, with a hint of nudity.

This is why the screwballs were so great at meet-cutes. With the thinly veiled innuendo of the Hays Code era and the crackling energy of the material, these meet-cutes are propulsive. The meet-cutes of later rom-coms sometimes strain to match the charm of their predecessors.

Katharine Hepburn's glittering dress will rip, forcing one of the meet-cutes in *Bringing Up Baby* (1938).

bottoms. Maybe they are antagonists like Hepburn and Grant in *Bringing Up Baby*. Whatever it is, there's that crackle of coincidence that means these two people who might have never crossed paths in a different universe are suddenly each other's only option.

PERFECT ROM-COM MOMENT
WHAT'S UP, DOC? (1972)

Peter Bogdanovich's *What's Up, Doc?* isn't so much of a send-up of classic screwballs as it is just a later addition to the canon. Just look to the early scene where Barbra Streisand's daffy dame Judy Maxwell encounters Ryan O'Neal's uptight

ABOVE: Peter Bogdanovich, Ryan O'Neal, and Barbra Streisand on the set of *What's Up, Doc?*, where she plays an irrepressible screwball.

musicologist in a hotel drugstore in San Francisco. She's irrepressible. Every time he takes something off a shelf, she's there peering at him through the next aisle over. She can jabber on about rocks and come up with scenarios off the top of her head at a moment's notice. She's trouble, surely. She invents a story for the cashier that they are husband and wife and calls him Steve. But she's also charming—a bubbly loony tune of a person. He's annoyed, and yet it's clear that she's going to win him over.

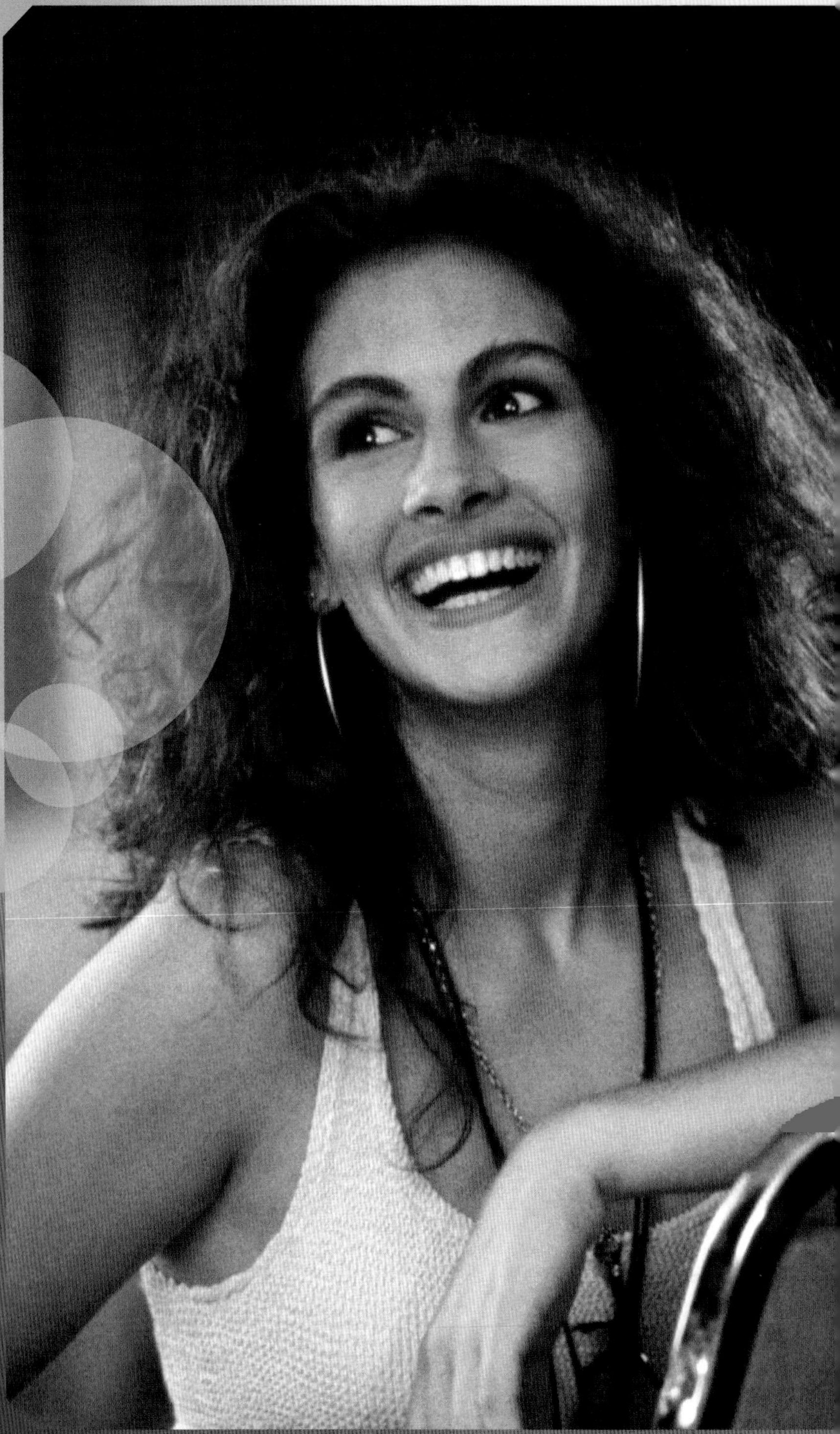

CHAPTER

3

AMERICA'S SWEETHEARTS

THE MODERN HOLLYWOOD STAR SYSTEM ISN'T QUITE BUILT for the rom-com. Rom-coms, for the most part, are based on personality, while these days, with a few exceptions, stars are made because they get a role in a franchise. Jennifer Lawrence had an Oscar nomination by the time she was cast in *The Hunger Games* (2012), but she became famous for playing Katniss Everdeen in the movie based on the popular YA novel. Still, Lawrence won her Academy Award for *Silver Linings Playbook* (2012), basically a rom-com, even though it was not marketed exactly as such, where she plays an unstable widow who convinces a mentally ill man (Bradley Cooper) to help her compete in a dance competition. In the past, Lawrence's career could have been entirely shaped by rom-coms. Instead, she became an action star first and then made rom-coms second.

Despite this very modern beginning, Lawrence has antecedents in the world of iconic rom-com stars. Lawrence's star persona has been compared to that of Carole Lombard, another celebrity whose image was centered on outspokenness and mixing glamour with a

OPPOSITE: Julia Roberts in *Pretty Woman* (1990).

down-to-earth "realness." The essayist Anne Helen Petersen wrote a piece aligning the two because of their perceived "cool girl" status. Lombard, however, reigned in the world of the screwball rom-com. She had an entrancing dizzy mania and a regality that made her the perfect heroine for the age. Even if you didn't always believe in the romances, you believed in her madcap energy.

It's a classic example of how, more so than their male counterparts, women rule the rom-com. Women's desirability is on full display in the romantic comedy, in part because Hollywood cinema was largely defined for years by male filmmakers. The audience should want to fall in love with the woman on-screen in the same way her costar does. (The same happens in reverse, but less frequently so. The man doesn't have to be quite so alluring. Meg Ryan always twinkles more than Tom Hanks or Billy Crystal.)

At the same time, a woman leading a rom-com must also be appealing to other women, who are often the intended audience of the movie. That means the star must be relatively unthreatening—you should want to be friends with her. Maybe you're a little intimidated, sure, but at the end of the day it's about being in her presence. Even if, say, you know you would never be able to be friends with multimillionaire pop star Jennifer Lopez in real life, you feel an attainable camaraderie when she's on-screen playing a wedding planner. That is the magic of this particular brand of star. The actresses who can be rom-com goddesses or American Sweethearts are part of a rarified group, but knowing who they are over the years is crucial to understanding the appeal and the staying power of the rom-com.

I like to think there are two categories by which we can divide these stars: Spitfires and Relatable Queens. The Spitfire knocks you off your feet the moment she walks in the door. She can't be contained and at first might seem a little overwhelming. The Spitfire seduces and puts you under her spell. By the time she is done with you, you are powerless to resist her charms.

The Relatable Queen, meanwhile, makes you feel comfortable immediately. You're in her world and it's a joy to be there. She is easy-going and sometimes a little undervalued. If you take a close look, you'll realize that she's incredibly glamorous—she's a movie star, after all—but when you're watching her you feel like you know someone like her, or maybe you even are her.

For the performers in question, making a career out of starring in rom-coms can be a blessing and a curse. Becoming a Sweetheart means entering a contract with the moviegoing public. To paraphrase the words of *Notting Hill*: You're just a girl, standing in front of a camera, asking the world to love you.

The most identifiable rom-com heroine is the one most easy to iden-tify with: the Relatable Queen. Meg Ryan, for instance, is a Relatable Queen and may be the case study for all rom-com heroines. But Jen-nifer Lopez, despite being an untouchable celebrity in real life, is also a Relatable Queen when she's in rom-coms. So is another musician-turned-movie star, Queen Latifah. It's a strange dynamic that only exists in Hollywood: To be a Relatable Queen on-screen one does not need to be a Relatable Queen in real life. Instead, on-screen you just need to project a sense that you are an everywoman, no matter how regal you might be otherwise.

In some sense, every rom-com star must be appealing to audi-ences in a way that might be defined as relatability, but the Relatable Queen makes it her essence. She is not boring, but she is not partic-ularly confrontational either. While the Spitfire is often humbled, the Relatable Queen must learn to stand up for herself and we, as the audience, rejoice as she does.

The Relatable Queen has been with us since the inception of the genre, and an early example is Jean Arthur. Arthur's name doesn't come up in rom-com conversations as much as some of her contem-poraries, despite her importance to the genre. The *Chicago Tribune*,

Jean Arthur in the fur coat that fell from the sky in *Easy Living* (1937).

writing on her eightieth birthday in 1985, called her America's "forgotten actress." That, in some ways, was by her own design. Arthur eschewed the press for much of her life. Some of her most famous roles were in dramas like Frank Capra's *Mr. Smith Goes to Washington* (1939) or George Stevens's western *Shane* (1953). But she was also a great romantic-comedy heroine, often playing women in over their heads who are forced to choose between two men. She played accomplished, smart gals, who were either struggling or solidly middle class. Her characters work for a living, and even though her heyday was in the '30s and '40s, these are thoroughly modern figures. In Mitchell Leisen's wacky 1937 screwball *Easy Living*, written by Preston Sturges, she is fired from her job at an austere magazine for boys when she unwittingly receives a fur coat thrown from the apartment of a wealthy banker, frustrated by his wife's excessive spending. In a bizarre turn of events, Arthur is mistaken for the rich man's mistress and installed in a suite by a hotelier who wants publicity. She's still poor, though, and while trying to scrape a meal together at the Automat, she meets the son of her benefactor, who is trying to make it on his own. They hit it off.

It's a perfect encapsulation of Arthur's powers. She is equally believable as an office worker and a glamour-puss, making the cases of mistaken identity all the more believable.

As the critic Kim Morgan wrote in an essay for *Criterion*, Arthur is "likely much more world-weary than you thought, a lot more intelligent, and much less virginal." Morgan writes "than you thought" because at first Arthur can come off a little prim. Her voice is high in a way that may make her appear uptight. In George Stevens's *The More the Merrier* (1943), she plays a Washington, D.C., government worker who rents out a room in her flat to an older gentleman played by Charles Coburn. She doesn't really want to share a space with a man, but she relents because of the World War II housing crisis, which has brought throngs to the district looking to pitch in for the cause. Arthur's Connie Milligan has a strict set of rules for her lifestyle—emphasized by her exacting morning routine—but she finds herself disarmed by the arrival of another man into her abode. Her new roommate offers up half of *his* room to a soldier named Joe Carter, played by Joel McCrea. As Connie falls more and more for Joe Carter, her controlling facade begins to slip away. So does her interest in her fiancé, who has strung her along for years.

That persona slippage also happens in *The Talk of the Town* (1942), another Stevens picture, in which Arthur plays a small-town girl housing a fugitive, played by Cary Grant, while also renting out her house to a law professor, portrayed by Ronald Colman. In one sequence, the professor finds her, wearing his borrowed pajamas, cooing to herself in a mirror.

Jean Arthur giving herself a sexy pep talk in *The Talk of the Town* (1942).

While the off-screen demeanor of rom-com stars is often as crucial to their image as the on-screen one, that was not the case for Arthur, who was an extremely private person. We do know, as Morgan recounts, that she was a perfectionist and probably something of a feminist, even if she didn't use those terms. She wrote in a 1936 essay that "Women would have been emancipated long ago if it hadn't been for the tyranny of the 'ladylike,' a false ideal and standard of deportment." Perhaps it's her ambivalence toward the whole Hollywood ecosystem that made Arthur such a good fit for rom-coms. She was distinct, and yet you could still project yourself onto her character's desires.

I see a lot of Jean Arthur in the women of the rom-com who would follow her, among them Diane Keaton and Meg Ryan. These are women who at first may seem buttoned-up, but who have a surprising sensuality. They are urban and wily, but also modest—at least at first glance—and unassuming.

Keaton and Ryan are easily smushed together because, stylistically, Ryan's breakout rom-com role owes so much to Keaton's. Without Annie Hall, there would be no Sally Albright. And early in Keaton's career her status as a rom-com queen was largely attributed to her working relationship with Allen. In the 2000s, though, she reclaimed her place as a rom-com heroine thanks to Nancy Meyers, who made her a mature woman's sex symbol in *Something's Gotta Give*, a 2003 movie wherein she sheds her turtleneck for an affair with Jack Nicholson. Even so, Keaton's career was never fully defined by rom-coms the way Ryan's was. Perhaps because before she was Annie Hall, she was Al Pacino's wife, Kay, in *The Godfather* (1972). As a result, she was always seen as a more versatile actress than Ryan—despite Ryan's own range. And yet Ryan remains the perennial ideal of the rom-com heroine, thanks to her efforts in Ephron's work.

Ryan was and is a savvier star than people give her credit for. Asked about the term "America's Sweetheart" in a 2019 *New York Times* interview, she said, "It doesn't allow for the full expression of a person. But that's what movie stardom is. There's a blankness required." Ephron cast Ryan as an avatar for herself in a way, except this avatar was one that was more palatable to every moviegoer. Ryan was her prettier—less New York-y—alter ego. Somehow it worked. Ryan could never quite explain why. "At times we would look at each other like, *Hmm*," Ryan told the *Times*.

Ephron saw something in Ryan that the press was sometimes reluctant to recognize. In Ephron's films, Ryan had an edge. She was sexual. Ryan could even be mean in Ephron's movies, as when she finally learns to icily take down Tom Hanks in *You've Got Mail* (1998).

Though Meg Ryan may be the queen of the Relatable Queens, others followed in her image, adding their own spin. Drew Barrymore emerged from child stardom as a heroine with an off-kilter energy, making her endearing as an undercover journalist reliving her high school nightmares in *Never Been Kissed* (1999) or as an amnesiac opposite Adam Sandler in *50 First Dates* (2004). Katherine Heigl's breakout role on television in *Grey's Anatomy* led to Judd Apatow casting her in *Knocked Up* (2007), which she followed up with *27 Dresses* (2008). Heigl's star was on the rise as the rom-com was falling from grace, and Heigl followed suit with her own set of controversies, despite her strong work on-screen.

But one Relatable heroine emerged just after Ryan who was maybe the most Relatable of them all: Sandra Bullock. And while Ryan is always, frankly, adorable on-screen in her rom-coms, in Bullock's first major rom-com she is a genuine sad sack.

Between 1994 and 1995, Sandra Bullock exploded onto the Hollywood scene with the release of her action movie *Speed* (1994) and her rom-com *While You Were Sleeping* (1995), a Jon Turteltaub production that cast Bullock as a truly lowly figure: Lucy, a lonely ticket taker on the Chicago L who saves the life of a (gorgeous) straphanger who falls on the tracks and just so happens to be her longtime crush. At the hospital she's mistaken for his fiancée and goes along with the ruse. Eventually she starts to fall for her fake lover's brother (Bill Pullman).

The character of Lucy is truly a schlub, with messy hair and oversized ugly sweaters, but the *New York Times*'s Janet Maslin immediately saw that Bullock might have a place in the pantheon. "A shy heroine in the gorgeous-wallflower tradition, she drowns in oversized clothing as Annie Hall did and seems in a perpetual state of comic dishevelment," Maslin wrote. "Forever covering her mouth bashfully or shrugging off life's affronts to her dignity, she has trouble only with being too radiant for her character's supposed mousiness." Indeed,

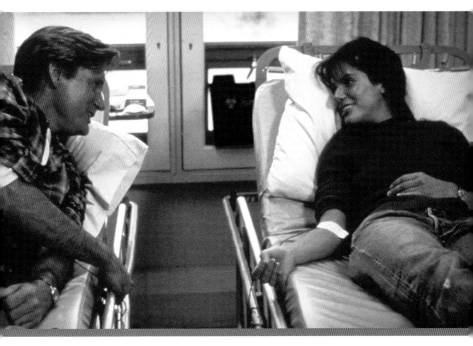

Bill Pullman and Sandra Bullock in *While You Were Sleeping* (1995).

Bullock's ability to shrink herself into that dishevelment, despite being a consummate movie star, would recur time and again in her filmography. A surprising number of Bullock's rom-coms involve some sort of transformation. In *Miss Congeniality* (2000) she's an FBI agent who goes undercover at a Miss USA pageant and needs to, therefore, learn to be a beauty queen. In *Two Weeks Notice* (2002) she's a hippie lawyer trying to save a community center from being torn down by Hugh Grant's ruthless businessman. At first, she's the kind of woman who wears ill-fitting suits and has unflattering bangs, until she's forced to dress up for a nice party. Even as recently as 2022 Bullock was playing this game. As a romance novel writer in *The Lost City*, her team encourages her to squeeze into an extremely tight, pink, sparkly jumpsuit for a book event, which becomes her uniform when she gets kidnapped—the joke being that she's incredibly uncomfortable and awkward in the form-fitting outfit.

In *Miss Congeniality* (2000), Sandra Bullock underwent one of her many transformations.

In these movies, Bullock enters a kind of contract with the audience—one that is inherent to the genre of rom-coms. We're supposed to ignore the fact that she's strikingly beautiful so we can see ourselves in her. It's an agreement the audience makes with a number of rom-com stars. When Renée Zellweger famously gained weight to play Bridget Jones in *Bridget Jones's Diary* (2001), it was to convince the viewers that she could stand to lose a few pounds just like the rest of us. (Even though she would quickly return to her previously svelte form and didn't even gain much weight to begin with.)

But there's no better example of this than the rom-com arc of Jennifer Lopez. Jennifer Lopez began her career as a Fly Girl dancer on TV's *In Living Color*, became a movie star playing pop star Selena Quintanilla (in 1997's *Selena*), and then became a giant pop star herself. Does it really make sense that we're supposed to see Lopez as an overworked wedding planner or a struggling maid? Not really. But that's the way the rom-com cookie crumbles—to butcher a quote from *The Apartment*. Lopez's early rom-com work positioned her as the underdog and, in two key instances, the employee. Both *The Wedding Planner* (2001) and *Maid in Manhattan* (2002) place Lopez's characters in service of their love interests. When it comes to the former, Lopez is responsible for arranging the nuptials of her would-be partner (Matthew McConaughey). In the latter, she's a domestic worker in the hotel where the Republican politician (Ralph Fiennes) she eventually falls for is staying.

As time went on, Lopez's roles got sleeker. By 2022, in *Marry Me*, she was essentially portraying herself: a wildly successful pop star whose private life is the subject of constant scrutiny. So why was Lopez positioned early on as a Relatable figure? It might have had something to do with the fact that, as a Latina, she was already defying the preestablished conventions of the rom-com star.

The world of the rom-com is dominated by white actresses. As a Latina entering those spaces, Lopez was inherently an outsider so Hollywood made her fit the types of spaces they thought she would occupy. While Black rom-com stars like Sanaa Lathan were frequently

Jennifer Lopez's characters were often put in service of their love interests, like in *Maid in Manhattan* (2002).

cast in movies that catered largely to Black audiences, Lopez was trying to enter the game dominated by Bullock and Ryan. If she were to play opposite Matthew McConaughey, she had to be his alternate choice. If she were to be wooed by a handsome politician, she had to be the maid, rather than the princess. At this point in Lopez's career, her accessibility was her superpower. She held herself like the superstar that she was, but she also made a hit song out of explaining how she was still just "Jenny from the block." These roles fit in with that lyric as well. She is trying to tell her public that this is her true self—all the glitz is just window dressing.

If a rom-com star doesn't happen to fit the mold of what a rom-com star should look like, Hollywood has a way of trying to make excuses for them. That's the case with Queen Latifah in a movie like *Just Wright* (2010).

In general, the world of Black rom-coms is often undervalued by both critics and Hollywood, despite being wildly popular with audiences.

Common and Queen Latifah in *Just Wright* (2010).

Regina Hall with Sanaa Lathan in *The Best Man Holiday* (2013).

Movies like *Brown Sugar* (2002) and *The Best Man* series, which began with the 1999 film of that title, established the likes of Sanaa Lathan, Nia Long, and Latifah as stars in the genre. Lathan's work in Gina Prince-Bythewood's *Love & Basketball* (2000)—which straddles the rom-com and rom-dram lines—is some of the best romantic acting in cinematic history. As a high school basketball player who is serious about her sport and ends up falling for her childhood best friend, who himself is pursuing a career in hoops, she's fierce yet utterly vulnerable. In *Brown Sugar* she also ends up in a romance with a guy she's known since childhood, in a reframing of a "girl next door" narrative. Meanwhile in *Something New* (2006), Lathan plays an accountant—perhaps the most boring rom-com job you can have—whose ideas for what she wants in a relationship are challenged when she falls for a white landscaper. Not only did she assume she wanted a Black man, she assumed she wanted someone of the same socioeconomic status as her, and instead he's below her. In *The Best Man*, Lathan is the reliable option for Taye Diggs. She plays the chef he's dating, who is threatened by his college flame, played by Nia Long.

But what about Queen Latifah, whose rap career established her as a challenger to the male-dominated musical establishment?

In *Just Wright*, Latifah is Leslie Wright—hence the title—a physical therapist who lives in New Jersey and is a massive fan of the pro basketball team the New Jersey Nets. One night after a game she has a meet-cute with star player Scott McKnight (Common) at a gas station. But when she goes to his birthday party on his invitation, she's overshadowed by her longtime friend Morgan (Paula Patton), who is gorgeous and out to nab herself an NBA husband. Scott proposes quickly to Morgan. Morgan, however, bolts when he gets injured, leaving Leslie to help Scott recuperate and prompting them to fall in love.

Latifah can vamp it up with the best of them. She evokes an Old Hollywood screen siren in *Chicago* (2002), the Best Picture–winning musical. But she also doesn't have a "typical" body for Hollywood love interests. So, she had to be a regular girl, compared to a bombshell like Patton. In *Just Wright* she's the consummate everywoman, who still gets the guy at the end.

That's what the Relatable Queen of the rom-com sells you on: You can be just like her. You don't have to be as cute as Meg Ryan or as charismatic as Queen Latifah, but you can still win the man of your dreams. They are stand-ins for the audience members, giving the viewers the hope and comfort that rom-coms so often provide.

Then who is the Spitfire? She is Claudette Colbert showing off her leg to hitch a ride in 1934's *It Happened One Night*. She is Barbara Stanwyck making Henry Fonda go limp in *The Lady Eve* (1941). She is Carole Lombard throwing a fit in *Twentieth Century* (1934).

But she is also Julia Roberts telling a salesgirl that she made a big mistake—nay, a *huge* mistake—in *Pretty Woman* (1990). She is Reese Witherspoon telling off a creepy professor in *Legally Blonde* (2001). She is Kate Hudson deceiving Matthew McConaughey in *How to Lose a Guy in 10 Days* (2003).

The Spitfire has edge. She's not afraid to toy with your emotions to get what she wants, though, of course, she has a sweet side underneath. She's sexy, and she knows how to use that to her advantage.

There is no fixed line dividing the Spitfire from the Relatable Queen. There are Spitfires who can morph into Relatable Queens and vice versa. "America's Sweetheart" can apply to both types. And yet, as popular as, say, Roberts was in her heyday, it's hard to ever imagine yourself in her shoes. And therein lies the distinction between these two rom-com archetypes.

If there's one thing that divides these two figures, it's sex. It's surprising that the Relatable Queen is sexual—even though she is. The Spitfire oozes sensuality upon first glance.

A headline in a 1934 edition of the *Los Angeles Times* blared: "Sex Appeal Just 'Hooey'—Claudette Colbert." It's a tantalizing quote, but as with many headlines it's a little misleading. Edwin Schallert writes: "If anybody were to be designated as having 'sex appeal' from the conventional Hollywood standpoint, it would be Claudette." Colbert, however, was arguing that you cannot fake sex appeal. She said on a radio show: "Charm is much more important than any so-called sex appeal. A person can even have a face like an ax and be possessed of charm. And it isn't something to be obviously 'turned on' either. There is nothing that I would hate more than just coming out in beautiful clothes and turning on the charm on the screen, or stage; that isn't acting as far as I'm concerned, and certainly it has no particular place in life."

In this one conversation, Colbert quickly summarizes what makes a star a star. She argues that an actor must appeal to those of every gender regardless of who they are sexually attracted to. (It was the 1930s, so she probably wasn't thinking about the wide spectrum of sexuality, but the point still stands.) "Personal magnetism and sex appeal aren't the same thing," she says. What Colbert doesn't say is that magnetism can be inherently sexy, and frequently the Spitfire wields it almost like a weapon.

Claudette Colbert flashing her leg for a ride in *It Happened One Night* (1934).

Just about a month before this article came out, Colbert flashed her leg in *It Happened One Night*—maybe the perfect example of how sex and charisma make a potent combination. That glimpse of skin isn't just great because it's scandalous. It's great because of how it utterly befuddles Clark Gable's Peter Warne. Colbert's Ellie Andrews takes matters into her own hands—or legs—and gets them where they need to go with her wiles, and, yes, a little bit of sex.

That hint of leg reverberates through time in performances by actresses who are Colbert's contemporaries as well as ones who follow her long into the future.

When I spoke to Aline Brosh McKenna, the writer behind many rom-coms and rom-com–adjacent projects, including *27 Dresses* and *The Devil Wears Prada* (2006), she compared Reese Witherspoon to Colbert. "She has that almost deceptively adorable face, which Claudette does as well," Brosh McKenna said. (Witherspoon starred in Brosh McKenna's 2023 rom-com *Your Place or Mine*.)

But there's more than just a facial similarity between Colbert and Witherspoon. There's an overarching sense of capability that they bring to their roles. Think, in the case of Witherspoon, of something

Reese Witherspoon strutting through Harvard in *Legally Blonde* (2001).

like *Legally Blonde*. The whole concept behind *Legally Blonde*, released in 2001, is that Witherspoon, as Elle Woods, from the outside looks like a vapid sorority girl and yet she's maybe the most competent woman on the planet. Not only can she get into Harvard Law School, but she can also succeed there if she puts her to mind to it. She doesn't abandon her sexuality or sense of fun, but she resents those (like the lascivious professor played by Victor Garber) who only see her for that. On the flip side, Witherspoon excels at playing haughty characters, another angle the Spitfire can take. In *Sweet Home Alabama* (2002), she's a woman who has rejected her country roots for the guise of a sleek New Yorker and is humbled when she has to head back down South.

Both these Witherspoon ladies are a spin on any number of roles played by Colbert, including in *It Happened One Night*, where Gable's Peter at first sees her as a silly heiress. He calls her a "brat," but she's the one who gets him out of scrapes. That same quality is there in Lubitsch's *Bluebeard's Eighth Wife* (1938). Gary Cooper's millionaire thinks Colbert's character, from a once-wealthy European family, will easily fall into his arms. Once she realizes that she's his eighth match, she cooks up a scheme via a prenuptial agreement. She can get a windfall if they split up, so she makes his life a living hell to ensure that will be the case. (As you might expect, she develops an affection for him, and though he ends up in a mental institution because of her high jinks, she comes back to him.) In *Midnight* from 1939, Colbert is a showgirl adrift in Paris who figures out a way to fend for herself. Time and again, Colbert proves her characters should never be underestimated, despite how they might first appear.

It helps that Colbert—and Witherspoon, for that matter—are cute as proverbial buttons, their round faces conveying a sweetness that can be deceptive in their pixie-like qualities. But they both possess the key quality of a Spitfire: They are not to be trifled with.

Claudette Colbert puts Gary Cooper in a straitjacket in *Bluebeard's Eighth Wife* (1938), directed by Ernst Lubitsch.

If Colbert could be deceptively competent, Barbara Stanwyck always made her intentions perfectly clear on-screen. It's arguably relevant that Stanwyck is as known for her work in rom-coms as she is for being a noir "femme fatale"—that ultimate example of mischievous feminine energy. Arguably her most famous performance is in Billy Wilder's 1944 *Double Indemnity*, playing a murderer who entraps an insurance salesman played by Fred MacMurray in her web of crime. But several of Stanwyck's rom-com roles have some of those same qualities, just reoriented for the humorous rather than the menacing.

Case in point: *The Lady Eve*. In what is her most famous screwball role, she plays a con artist, who first seduces Henry Fonda on a cruise, luring him into a card game to take his money. Then she falls in love, confesses everything, and he rejects her. To get back at him, she later decides to pose as a British aristocrat, the eponymous "Lady Eve." He is taken by this proper lady, only to be devastated when she reveals her sordid past, which lands him back in the arms of Stanwyck's original character, unaware that she is Lady Eve as well.

Stanwyck was poised and gorgeous, but you could also sense that she had lived a full and sometimes complicated life—which she had. Originally from Brooklyn—and named Ruby Stevens—she grew up an orphan after her mother died and her father abandoned the family. She had worked since she was a teenager, long before she made a career of acting. Her roles reflected her own gumption. She told the *New York Times* in a 1981 interview: "I couldn't stand being passive. I couldn't play the placid girl."

Once again, you can see a Stanwyckian influence throughout rom-com history. She's the woman who comes into a man's life and completely changes his worldview and perception. In *Ball of Fire* (1941), directed by Howard Hawks, she's a showgirl who goes by the name "Sugarpuss." Her coarse language fascinates a group of stodgy professors who all live together, including the handsome (but uptight) English professor Bertram, played by Gary Cooper. She leads the men into danger because of her affiliation with a mobster who wants to marry her, but she also breaks them out of their dull existence, especially in the case of Bertram.

Watching *Ball of Fire*, it's easy to see how Stanwyck's influence filtered down into the work and stardom of Julia Roberts. Roberts's prevailing image is thoroughly more wholesome than Stanwyck's, though perhaps without reason. She is the woman who defines the idea of the "American Sweetheart." In a 1999 profile of her for *Vanity Fair*, her friend Rupert Everett called her "Miss America." "She's

Barbara Stanwyck as a showgirl in *Ball of Fire* (1941).

got all the qualities that people want an American woman to have," he said.

By just focusing on Roberts as an all-American movie star, you remove the edge that's inherent in many of her performances, including in her rom-coms. There's a forcefulness to Julia Roberts's best work that you can take for granted if you just see her as that million-watt smile.

If *Ball of Fire* was a Hays Code–era "hooker with a heart of gold" movie, then *Pretty Woman* was a modern "hooker with a heart of gold" movie. Sure, maybe the Garry Marshall movie was sanded down from the original screenplay, and maybe Roberts's persona doesn't exactly scream "down-on-her-luck sex worker," but she makes it work just because of how much of a force she is. In the movie she wavers from vulnerable—her initial uncertainty with Beverly Hills luxury comes through in her frustration—to self-assured.

In *My Best Friend's Wedding* (1997), she took the charm and transformed it into something more insidious: a woman who would bully her male best friend's fiancée to get them to break up. Roberts pulls off a fascinating feat in *My Best Friend's Wedding*: Somehow she makes her character a person women *should* hate—someone who is truly mean to her fellow females—into someone you can sympathize with and root for. And that other woman is played by Cameron Diaz, a performer, who, within the two rom-com archetypes, fits into the Relatable Queen category for most of her career. She's strikingly pretty even as she maintains a goofy everywoman demeanor. In this film her main mode is sweetness, the ability overcoming the obstacles that Julia puts out for her at every turn with a mostly humble smile on her face.

Julia Roberts plotting Cameron Diaz's undoing in *My Best Friend's Wedding* (1997).

In many of her classic roles, we should hate Julia, but we somehow still love her. It's evident in one key scene from *Notting Hill*, a movie that came out at the peak of her fame in 1999. Invited to dinner with the friends of Hugh Grant's unassuming bookseller, Roberts's Anna Scott, a movie star not unlike Roberts herself, engages in a game to determine who has the saddest life. The other people participating have genuine hardships. One woman is in a wheelchair and can't have children. Another keeps dating bad men. But then Anna explains the challenges of being a celebrity whose every movement is judged, who is forced to go on soul-sucking diets and can't have any privacy. She almost convinces the group to pity her based on the power of her performance until they laugh her off.

Notting Hill understands that Julia Roberts's characters are maybe, secretly, at their core, sort of unlikable. But through her force of will, she can get you on their side.

≫——→ ♥ ←——≪

The Spitfire can be effortlessly cool, maybe to the point of coldness, but she can also be zany, unfettered by the bounds of normal human behavior. Katharine Hepburn at turns can be both these women. In *The Philadelphia Story* (1940) she's the wealthy Tracy Lord, set to marry a man who thinks of her as a goddess rather than a human. But in *Bringing Up Baby* (1938) she's Susan Vance, another rich girl, who is silly instead of cold. Susan is the kind of girl who adopts a leopard as a pet, never thinking of the consequences. In both films, Cary Grant eventually becomes smitten. Susan wears him down. Tracy, meanwhile, lets him in. They are completely different entities, but Hepburn's spirit links them.

It's impossible to overlook Hepburn, whomever she is inhabiting. Whether the daffy Susan or the confidently poised Tracy, she is still always Katharine Hepburn, with her mid-Atlantic lilt and striking bone structure. Hepburn was and still is renowned for testing the rules of gender even as she played roles in iconic romantic comedies.

Katharine Hepburn overwhelming John Howard in *The Philadelphia Story* (1940).

She famously wore pants at a time when that fashion choice was bold and unconventional. She relished and embraced androgyny, aware that she was playing life (and Hollywood) by her own rules. Tracy and Susan are both very feminine characters, but Hepburn's subversion runs through them. In her legendary 1981 interview with Barbara Walters, Hepburn said: "I have not lived as a woman. I have lived as a man. I've just done what I damn well wanted to and I made enough money to support myself, and I ain't afraid of being alone."

The other Hepburn, Audrey, often seems like she exists in contrast to Kate. Whereas Kate's fashion was masculine, Audrey was seen as an example of delicate femininity. And yet she too was a type of Spitfire. Audrey's roles often have a thread of nonconformity running through them, as is typical of Spitfires. Princess Ann in *Roman*

Holiday (1953) escapes to discover a world beyond her duties, cutting her hair short in the process. Sabrina in *Sabrina* (1954) refuses to resign herself to a life of service like her father. In *Funny Face*, from 1957, Audrey plays an oddball bohemian recruited into high-fashion modeling by a photographer played by Fred Astaire. And then, of course, in *Breakfast at Tiffany's* (1961) she's Holly Golightly, the greatest free spirit of them all, a woman who refuses to give her cat a name beyond "Cat" because she doesn't want him to feel possessed.

All rom-coms deal in gender roles, but the Spitfire is more likely to subvert them. Carole Lombard was keenly aware of these distinctions. In a 1937 issue of *Photoplay* magazine, the blonde star explained to her public "how I live by a man's code." The author of the

Audrey Hepburn doing a bohemian dance in *Funny Face* (1957).

article, Hart Seymore, was careful to highlight Lombard's feminine beauty even in discussing how she defied that. "Having found herself plumped down into a world where men are supposed to be masters of all creation, Carole has simply adapted herself to her surroundings. She lives her life on the logical premise that she has equal rights with the male of the species, but she (wise girl) preserves all her feminine prerogatives," he wrote. Answering the question about how she gets along "so well in a man's world," Lombard replied: "A woman has just as much right in the world as a man, and can get along in it just as well if she puts her mind to it."

In her performances, Lombard often played women who were, yes, distinctly feminine, but who could also barrel through their circumstances. When Howard Hawks's *Twentieth Century* begins, her character is an aspiring actress named Mildred Plotka, whom John Barrymore's director Oscar Jaffe wants to mold into a star, renaming

Carole Lombard trying to ingratiate herself with William Powell in *My Man Godfrey* (1936).

Kate Hudson sinks her teeth into Matthew McConaughey in *How to Lose a Guy in 10 Days* (2003)—with the help of a dog in a sweater.

her "Lily Garland." Once the action speeds ahead in time Lily *is* that star, and she has grown frustrated with Oscar, who is also now her boyfriend, and his controlling nature. Lily is a fabulous terror, but she also has every right to be angry at Oscar, so she wields her fame like a weapon. (Almost a decade later, in 1942, Lombard would play another vainglorious actress in *To Be or Not to Be*, using her feminine wiles to spy on the Nazis invading Poland.)

Lombard's effortless glamour could easily spill into lunacy, as in the case of *My Man Godfrey* (1936), where her ditzy heiress falls madly in love with the eponymous butler whom she employed in her household after finding him on the street. When they finally get married at the end, it's unclear if Godfrey actually enjoys spending time with Lombard's Irene or if she has just muscled her way into his life.

Lombard's work is renowned, and while it may not seem obvious at first glance, there's a connection between her work in *My Man Godfrey* and Kate Hudson's in *How to Lose a Guy in 10 Days*. And much like Lombard in her heyday, if there were a princess of the early to mid-2000s rom-com boom, it would be Kate Hudson.

Rom-coms are in Kate Hudson's DNA. Her mother, Goldie Hawn, is a rom-com icon in her own right. Hawn won an Oscar for *Cactus Flower* (1969), in which she played a lovelorn hippie fawning over Walter Matthau's dentist. As Hawn grew older her image evolved. She still had that charming smile, her mouth turned slightly upward, but her characters could be whiners and ladies who found themselves in over their heads. (In 1980's *Private Benjamin* she joins the army. In 1987's *Overboard* she falls off a boat and loses her memory.)

Her daughter Kate's movie stardom was almost predestined. "There's something that makes movie stars, and I think Kate Hudson has got that magic. I can't even say what it is, but you know when someone has it. She just lights up the scene—and the screen," the director Robert Altman said in a 2000 *Vanity Fair* profile. Hudson's first major role found her playing the "Band Aid" Penny Lane, who insists she's not a groupie, in Cameron Crowe's 1970s rock 'n' roll coming-of-age story *Almost Famous* (2000). Hudson has a certain sweetness about her that can distract from the bite she deploys. It's clear in *Almost Famous* why Penny is entrancing to the fifteen-year-old aspiring journalist who meets her, but she is elusive and sometimes callous to him, stringing him along as she pursues an affair with the older, mysterious guitarist. That's also true in 2003's *How to Lose a Guy in 10 Days*, the rom-com that cemented her superstardom. There, she's Andie Anderson, a columnist at the fictional *Composure* magazine, who sets out to write a column about the task posed in the title of the movie. She pegs advertising executive Benjamin Barry, played by Matthew McConaughey, as her mark. He, meanwhile, is on a mission to prove that he can make any woman fall in love with him. Fully aware of what she's doing, Hudson's Andie goes about playing the part of the desperate woman, torturing Ben by forcing him to miss sporting events he cares about and bringing a ridiculous-looking dog into his life. Given his own task, he refuses to give up, and both eventually let their guard down.

How to Lose a Guy in 10 Days is more frivolous than, say, *Twentieth Century* or *Bluebeard's Eighth Wife*, but the savviness that Hudson brings to the part recalls Lombard's sparkle or Colbert's guile. She's effervescently stunning when she comes out wearing a phenomenally tailored yellow dress but is also convincingly effective at portraying a woman being annoying for the sake of professional gain.

The key thing about the Spitfire is that you probably don't want to cross her. Sure, she'll be forgiving eventually, since that is the way these plots often go. But while the Relatable Queen emerges out of her shell, the Spitfire has personality that's already impossible to deny. She takes over rooms and bends the world to her liking. Just try resisting her—if you dare.

PERFECT ROM-COM MOMENT
IT HAPPENED ONE NIGHT (1934)

The first time heiress Ellie Andrews (Claudette Colbert) and journalist Peter Warne (Clark Gable) share a room in *It Happened One Night*, he erects what he calls the "walls of Jericho," referring to the biblical story. It's a blanket that divides their sleeping areas to give some sense of privacy. "Maybe not as thick as the ones that Joshua blew down with his trumpet," he says, "but a lot safer. You see, I have no trumpet." This is before they've fallen in love, so Ellie is suspicious of Peter's intentions, but there's something inevitably sexy about them sharing a room with so little dividing them. In the end, when they finally get married, Peter asks for a trumpet. As an audience we don't see that wall come down, but we hear the sounds of the horn, and we know what's happening.

CHAPTER

THE MEN

WHEN I SPOKE TO AMERICAN SCREENWRITER ALINE BROSH McKenna, she reflected on evolving attitudes of male stars toward rom-coms.

"You just would never question Clark Gable doing *It Happened One Night* [1934] and then turning around and doing a drama," she said. But in more recent decades, this concern that romantic comedies were not serious work seems to have taken hold of a broader swath of actors. The refrain she hears from a lot of male stars is that they won't do superhero movies (too passé at this point) and that they only want to work with the best directors. "For whatever reason that ends up never being women and never a movie where you show love for a woman."

This is an evolution of opinion that has a lot to do with the rise of superhero movies as a viable career path for actors, starting in 2008 with the success of *Iron Man* and *The Dark Knight*. Superhero movies drove many men away from rom-coms.

Look at, for instance, the career of Ryan Reynolds.

Reynolds, a Canadian with a knack for playing smug wiseacres, first started gaining traction in Hollywood as the star of romantic comedies. In *Just Friends* (2005) he played a now-successful former dork trying to win back his high school crush. In *Definitely, Maybe* (2008)

OPPOSITE: Hugh Grant in *About a Boy* (2002).

he's a guy recounting his former romances to his precocious young daughter. And, at the apex of his rom-com career, he starred opposite Sandra Bullock in *The Proposal* (2009) as an underling who is roped into a scheme, pretending he's engaged to his demanding boss.

But just two years after *The Proposal*, he was cast as Hal Jordan, the DC superhero, in *Green Lantern* (2011). *Green Lantern* was not a commercial success, but Reynolds got the comic book bug, and when he suited up again for *Deadpool* (2016) he finally had that hit he longed for. After scoring the role as the foul-mouthed mercenary Deadpool, Reynolds then moved away from rom-coms, opting for mostly action movies, cameos, or other potential franchises.

Another example of this trend is Paul Rudd. The seemingly ageless wonder has had many phases of his career. But he started out as a rom-com object of affection. He broke out in *Clueless* (1995) as the hunky college-aged ex-stepbrother of spoiled teen Cher Horowitz (Alicia Silverstone). Later he segued into supporting roles in Judd Apatow's run of foul-mouthed, male-centric rom-coms like *Knocked Up* (2007) before getting his own version of the form in *This Is 40* (2012). He even made fun of the rom-com and its tropes in *They Came Together* (2014). And then he became Ant-Man.

Both these scenarios are good indications of what, in the 2010s, became a common arc for a man's career in Hollywood. Of course, there is the chicken and the egg question. Was the industry not making romantic comedies because men didn't want to star in them? Or did men not want to star in romantic comedies because the industry wasn't making them? Or did another trend stifle the male desire to star in rom-coms?

We can identify that trend: The idea that young up-and-comers started to reject both rom-coms and superhero movies for something more ostensibly dramatically fulfilling.

Matthew McConaughey serves as a prime example of an actor who made this turn. In the early 2000s, he, alongside Kate Hudson, was one of the preeminent figures of the rom-com genre. And, as he wrote in his memoir *Greenlights*, he, for the most part, relished the role. He wasn't mad that his work wasn't critically well received, and he was happy with the paychecks he was getting. Still, he grew tired. He wrote: "One, the romantic comedies stopped presenting a challenge for me. I felt like I could read the script today and play the part tomorrow. Two, I was beginning to feel like an entertainer, not an actor." There's an argument to be made that McConaughey himself was underestimating the skill that came with making romantic comedies or that he wasn't picking the best of the bunch; nonetheless, his attitude is one that is commonplace. You are unlikely to win an Oscar for a rom-com—especially if you're a man.

But as romantic comedies continue to be made, holding a place in the hearts and minds of audiences, actors look to iconic film stars of decades past for inspiration. But who to emulate? There is one star who is the greatest of all of them in this respect.

≫──────▷ 🖤 ◁──────≪

The platonic ideal of a male rom-com star is Cary Grant. Born in Britain under the name Archibald Leach, on-screen Grant could be at turns debonair and zany, sincere and cynical. He was paired with a variety of partners, including Irene Dunne, Katharine Hepburn, Audrey Hepburn, Jean Arthur, and Rosalind Russell. They all held their own against him, but in the end, their characters were powerless to resist his gaze.

Obviously he was dashing, with a strong jaw and intense features—that goes without saying—but there was something else about him that just popped on-screen. Grant made being a romantic-comedy star look appealing and effortless. He carved a path that plenty of men would then follow, though, truthfully, nobody matched him. He could be the rogue, as he often was, or the honorable choice.

What was it about Grant? Was it the distinctive accent that could only be attributed to him? The tan skin and thick head of hair? The searching eyes? It was all that, yes, but also his ability to keep up with the energies of his partners on-screen, whether he was countering them, acting as a foil, or equaling their levels of mania.

Grant wasn't the first Hollywood leading man with a knack for romantic comedy. There were plenty who either preceded him or were his contemporaries. In fact, when Grant first arrived on the scene, at least one publication wrote about him as if he were simply an easy replacement for Gary Cooper. "Was Cary Grant being groomed to take Gary Cooper's place when the latter went abroad?" is what Jack Jamison wrote in a 1933 issue of *Photoplay* under the headline "Cary versus Gary." At the time, the idea was that Gary Cooper was passé and Paramount was calling Grant in from New York, where he was starring onstage. "Cary looks enough like Gary to be his brother," one caption read. "Both are tall, they weigh about the same, and they fit the same sort of roles. Even their names are similar!"

But Cooper's career was far from over, and he and Grant occupied different worlds in Hollywood. Cooper's stoicism would ultimately make him a great fit for westerns, and even in the romance space he would often play a towering man, clueless to his own beauty in films like *Ball of Fire* (1941) and *Bluebeard's Eighth Wife* (1938).

Not that the ascendancy of Grant was overstated. By the late 1930s *Screenland* published a story speculating that Grant was commanding $250,000 a picture. "Fact: Cary Grant is currently the most-in-demand freelance young leading man in films," the article stated. In 1938 he starred in not one but two films opposite Katharine Hepburn, who would become his most powerful on-screen partner—though Irene Dunne, who appeared with him in *The Awful Truth* (1937) and *My Favorite Wife* (1940), was another significant contender.

Hepburn and Grant, with their equally unplaceable dialectical flourishes that melded English diction with Americanisms, made a perfect team. But they also didn't repeat themselves when they paired up. In *Bringing Up Baby* (1938), easily the looniest of their films, she's

Cary Grant squabbling with Irene Dunne in *The Awful Truth* (1937).

the hopelessly in love ditz to his stressed-out paleontologist. In *Holiday* (1938), he's an interloper in a rich family, engaged to marry one woman but tempted to explore more of life by her free-spirited sister, played by Hepburn.

By 1940, he and Hepburn would release what would be their masterpiece: *The Philadelphia Story*. C. K. Dexter Haven may be the ultimate Grant character, and not just because of his perfect name. The first image we get of Haven is one that doesn't sit as well with modern audiences as it would have in 1940. In what constitutes a brief flashback, we see Dexter punch Hepburn's Tracy Lord in the face after she throws his golf clubs after him—a brief glance into the end of their marriage.

The action picks back up as Tracy is about to get married again to a boringly wealthy man with no real personality. (It's always one of those.) Dexter returns to the Lords' estate along with two journalists (Jimmy Stewart and Ruth Hussey) to help him get the scoop on the nuptials. Tracy is thoroughly unsettled by Dexter's presence, but she's also drawn to him. In their interactions you get the sense that they know each other deeply, despite their antagonism.

Grant's Dexter is savage to Tracy and her current situation. He goes after her for marrying rich and for what he perceives as her coldness. He says: "You'll never be a first-class human being or a first-class woman until you've learned to have some regard for human frailty. It's a pity your own foot can't slip a little sometime, but your sense of inner divinity wouldn't allow that." It's a brutal assessment that gets to her own insecurities. It should be unbearably mean—and it is to Tracy—but from Grant's mouth it also rings true. He brings Tracy, who we know can dish it out as well as she takes it, back down to earth.

Cary Grant and Katharine Hepburn facing off in *The Philadelphia Story* (1940).

Cary Grant as a knight in shining armor in *The Bachelor and the Bobby-Soxer* (1947).

It's a clever spin on the *Bringing Up Baby* dynamic, where she forces his reasonable character into her nutty schemes with such force that he can't resist.

Off-screen, Grant was married five times, and the press sold the idea of Grant as an eligible bachelor time and time again. In 1938 *Motion Picture* declared him "Public Bachelor No. 1." Then nine years later *Movieland* asked, "Are you the girl for Cary Grant?" In the story, Alyce Canfield wrote that there is "probably no Hollywood male more worthy of a glint in your eye than Cary. He has a head start on all the glamor boys. No scandal has ever touched him; he's never indulged in cheap little romances; he has lived his life in quiet good taste." It was then followed by a quiz designed to tell the reader whether she is indeed the one for Cary Grant.

The *Movieland* story teased Grant's upcoming appearance in the 1947 rom-com *The Bachelor and the Bobby-Soxer*, which, even in its title, plays into the idea that he is one to be scooped up. But there's a little wrinkle. He plays a devilish painter named Dick Nugent who catches the eye of a hormonal teen named Susan (Shirley Temple, grown up from the little tyke she was during her most famous roles). Susan's sister Margaret (Myrna Loy) is a strict judge who had recently encountered Dick in court. When Susan's infatuation won't stop, Margaret encourages Dick to start dating her little sister with the hopes that Susan will eventually see through him. Then the age-appropriate Dick and Margaret develop feelings for each other.

The plot feels a little outdated in the twenty-first century, with an adult man being asked to date a teenager, even if the resolution is all aboveboard. But it's an example of Cary Grant's appeal. To both Susan and Margaret, he appears as a literal knight in shining armor—they have visions of him gleaming in medieval garb—but he's also a cad. He's the kind of guy who frequents nightclubs and lands himself in court to settle squabbles. He's both a man who will save you, as both Margaret and Susan hope, and one who needs just a little bit of saving. That's Grant's specialty, and it's part of that ephemeral magic of a romantic comedy.

There have been plenty of men since Cary Grant who excelled in rom-coms. Rock Hudson's collaborations with Doris Day and beyond made him a hunk with a knack for subverting his masculine good looks with physical comedy. Jack Lemmon had a self-deprecating air that made him ideal for lovelorn pining. In rom-coms like *Roman Holiday* (1953) and *Designing Woman* (1957), Gregory Peck's gravitas allowed for the antics to whirl around him. In the 1970s George Segal carried the torch, bringing more of a streetwise energy to his trysts. And by the time we get to the 1980s and 1990s, Tom Hanks had started to emerge as the throwback star Hollywood was longing for—a man with the versatility of Grant or Clark Gable and the American nobility of Jimmy Stewart.

And yet it seems fitting that the most obvious heir to Cary Grant's throne would be from England and would also be named Grant.

In 1994, a bright new hope for the rom-com arrived across the pond in *Four Weddings and a Funeral*, the Richard Curtis–scripted

Hugh Grant being adorably sheepish in *Four Weddings and a Funeral* (1994).

film directed by Mike Newell. The man in question was slightly unkempt, but in an endearing way, his mop of hair falling into his eyes. It was Hugh Grant, and he would become a rom-com institution unto himself—though not without some hiccups along the way.

Comparisons to the classics, specifically to the other Grant, were almost immediate. In a *New York Times* article titled "Hugh Grant Makes Them Think of Cary Grant," John Duigan, his director in the film *Sirens* (1994), explained: "Hugh has the capacity to be a terrific player of light comedy, in the tradition of Cary Grant and David Niven." That same year, the *Washington Post* explained that his work "has drawn critical kudos and giddy comparisons to Cary Grant."

While *Four Weddings and a Funeral* was not exactly Grant's debut—there were other films like the aforementioned *Sirens* or the Merchant-Ivory drama *Maurice* (1987) that made people take notice—it was the one that cemented his reputation as a rom-com staple. In the opening scene his character Charles is late for one of the eponymous celebratory affairs. He is a mess, but that mess is just so adorable.

There's a trick that Newell and Curtis pull off. It's naturally a bit ridiculous to think that Hugh Grant would be so unlucky in love, but the filmmakers make it clear that he is not *not* desired. His best friend Fiona (Kristin Scott Thomas) harbors feelings for him; his ex (Anna Chancellor), whom Fiona calls Duckface, is still smitten with him; and the mysterious American Carrie, played by Andie MacDowell, immediately invites him up to her bedroom in an inn, even if she does eventually get married to a rich Scotsman. Yet, Grant is so intentionally hangdog, so adorably sheepish, that he's believable as a man of romantic misfortune. But the slip in that perfectly charming persona also allowed for interesting wrinkles in his on-screen presence. Yes, he would still play delightful Englishmen who stumble over their words, as in *Notting Hill* (1999*)*, where he's the humble bookseller to Julia Roberts's movie star. But the *Bridget Jones* movies, other Richard Curtis–penned productions, introduced the idea of Grant as a

Hugh Grant wooing Rachel Weisz after learning some life lessons in *About a Boy* (2002).

desirable jerk. He's sexy and sex-obsessed in the movie, luring the heroine into a sordid intraoffice affair and then ditching her when it's convenient. Daniel Cleaver in *Bridget Jones* is ultimately a bad guy, but other Grant characters simply need to be a little reformed.

As Grant aged, his rom-com parts leaned into this complexity. The first film beyond *Bridget Jones* that really used this to its full effect was *About a Boy* (2002), which casts Grant as Will Freeman, a perennial bachelor living off the royalties from a holiday song his dad wrote. For dates, he chases single moms by pretending to have a child and going to a support group. Will actively avoids relationships but ends up getting sucked into hanging around with an awkward kid (Nicholas Hoult) whose mother is a friend of one of the women Will is seeing. The *rom* part of this rom-com is almost secondary, though it is there when he starts wooing another mom, played by Rachel Weisz. The pleasure is less about the love story, as was the case in *Four Weddings* and *Notting Hill*. It is about watching him become a better person, a romantic fantasy in its own way.

He continued down a path of self improvement on-screen. *Two Weeks Notice* (2002) cast him as a playboy billionaire who doesn't care about others until he is assisted by an advocacy lawyer played by Sandra Bullock. Then they find mutual attraction and he grows a heart. In *Music and Lyrics* (2007) he's a washed-up pop star who collaborates with an up-and-coming songwriter played by Drew Barrymore. Even in *Love Actually* (2003) he's the buttoned-up prime minister who has eschewed love until an attractive new employee crosses his path.

The other Grant—Cary—was even more widely known for work outside the genre. He was equally well regarded for his work in Hitchcock suspense films like *North by Northwest* (1959) and *To Catch a Thief* (1955). Hugh was perhaps more pigeonholed, and yet they share a romantic dominance. Both can be devastatingly suave and yet not so refined that they don't seem like real people. The fantasy of them is in their bite.

If Cary Grant has a foil in *The Philadelphia Story*, it's not the guy who plays Hepburn's boring husband-to-be, George Kittredge (John Howard), it's Jimmy Stewart as Mike Connor, the reporter who is there to get a gossipy tabloid story about the event. Grant and Stewart are polar opposites. Grant is the rakish Brit with a twinkle in his eye; Stewart exudes all-American earnestness with a dash of hard-won cynicism.

In the film, Mike arrives at the Lords' estate with an axe to grind about the rich. He's an everyman in the sense that he has an everyman's disdain for the whims of the wealthy. And yet he finds himself immediately taken with Tracy, and she's intrigued by him too. He's a different kind of person than she's used to dealing with: He's a bit

Jimmy Stewart and Jean Arthur in *You Can't Take It with You* (1938).

crass and a bit common and definitely gets way too drunk, but that's also sort of appealing.

Mike gets chucked over by Tracy eventually when she goes back to Grant's C. K. Dexter Haven, but he still gets a romance in the end: the sarcastic photographer Elizabeth Imbrie (Ruth Hussey), who has been patiently waiting for him with a roll of her eyes. In plenty of his other rom-com roles, Stewart is no second fiddle, however.

While arguably best known for his earnest work in *Mr. Smith Goes to Washington* (1939) or *It's a Wonderful Life* (1946), Stewart was also a unique rom-com lead. He wasn't as suave as some of his contemporaries and was less of a traditional heartthrob, with his thin face and sometimes goofy air, but he could also be a match for Jean Arthur (1938's *You Can't Take It with You*), Margaret Sullavan (1940's *The Shop Around the Corner*), and Kim Novak (1958's *Bell, Book and Candle*). The thing about Stewart's rom-com heroes is they could be perceived as jerks, as in *The Shop Around the Corner*, or pushovers, as in *Bell, Book and Candle*, but there was always something sort of brilliantly normal about them. In *You Can't Take It with You*, that's the whole point. His love's family is full of zany people, and he's the regular guy thrust into it. You would be hard-pressed to find a Cary Grant in the wild, but there's a chance you might meet a Jimmy Stewart.

It's of course the same quality that helped propel Tom Hanks to rom-com fame in the 1980s and 1990s. At this point saying Tom Hanks is the modern-day Jimmy Stewart is like saying water is wet or the grass is green. It's a comparison that's been made throughout Hanks's career, and one that Hanks has both embraced and countered. He once said, "It's as big a compliment as you can get, but it's not anywhere near accurate."

The Hanks-Stewart comparison is not simply because of rom-coms. In fact, it has more to do with the two of them standing in as a cinematic arbiter of American goodness time and time again. But their rom-com performances are also comparable—even beyond the obvious fact that *You've Got Mail* (1998) is a remake of *The Shop Around the Corner*. Hanks is not an actor audiences ever really lusted after in the same way Jimmy Stewart was not. Even in his young roles he played silly more than sexy. (The fact that 1988's *Big*, in which he plays a kid trapped in a grown man's body after a wish gone wrong, has a romantic element has always been a little creepy, even though Hanks manages to sell it.)

Hanks's best rom-com work combines charm, prickliness, and relatability. In *Sleepless in Seattle* (1993), women around the country start swooning over him because of the impassioned memory of his wife he delivers over the radio. But he's not eager to take his adoring fans up on their offers of company. He's finicky, and rightfully so. There's a similar vibe he gives off in *You've Got Mail*. Joe Fox is a

Tom Hanks and Elizabeth Perkins in *Big* (1988).

ruthless businessman, but also a good caregiver to his younger relatives. It's his interactions with those kids that makes Meg Ryan take notice, before she realizes they are feuding. Hanks has that stratospheric charm, but in a package that makes him seem like a person you might encounter in real life. He makes the most absurd scenarios (see 1988's *Big,* 1984's *Splash,* and both the Nora Ephron titles) believable by bringing them down-to-earth.

With the Grants—Cary and Hugh—you get a pure fantasy. With Stewart and Hanks you get a version of reality. A movie star version, of course, but a version nonetheless.

PERFECT ROM-COM MOMENT
NOTTING HILL (1999)

The part that is most often forgotten about the famous "I'm just a girl" moment from *Notting Hill* is that it ends in a rejection. Julia Roberts's Anna Scott arrives at the bookstore of Hugh Grant's William Thacker asking for a second chance at a

ABOVE: Julia Roberts is "just a girl" in *Notting Hill* (1999).

relationship. Her voice quakes from the minute she walks in the door. She knows what she's doing is risky. She's a movie star used to being in front of a crowd, but putting herself out there right now is the most vulnerable thing she could possibly do. But the catch is, William says no to her offer. He's had his heart broken by her before and worries that she's not sincere. After all, he just accidentally heard her brushing him off to a fellow actor, which she says he misunderstood without context.

So he rejects her, and she makes one more plea. She's not the untouchable celebrity he made her out to be. She's "just a girl, standing in front of a boy, asking him to love her." It should work instantly, but it doesn't. It's not until later that William realizes what a nincompoop he has been. And yet the fact that it doesn't register makes it all the more meaningful. She's just laid her heart out. He's failed to see that, and he's going to have to atone.

CHAPTER

5

(PERFECT (PAIRS

THE GREATEST STARS OF THE ROM-COM CAN SPARKLE against whomever they are opposite, but there is a specific alchemical event that happens when the movies match up a couple who thrive in each other's presence. These are the perfect pairs of the rom-com, the couples audiences keep coming back to see because when they are together, they are something special.

They are the names that immediately leap to mind when you think about cinematic pairings: Katharine Hepburn and Spencer Tracy; Doris Day and Rock Hudson; Tom Hanks and Meg Ryan. The trick is that they work together in any context. Sure, they tend to replay some beats movie to movie, but the effect is something sparkly every single time—even if the movies vary in quality.

So how in love should stars actually be to project love on-screen?

Katharine Hepburn and Spencer Tracy made nine films together, far more than any other pair I discuss in this book. Not all of them were romantic comedies, though the ones they are most remembered for are. The Hepburn and Tracy pictures are often battle-of-the-sexes stories, in which Hepburn plays an accomplished woman who is nevertheless tested by Tracy's blue-collar roughnecks.

OPPOSITE: Rock Hudson and Doris Day.

Here's where I'll admit something that's probably unfashionable. I've never been a huge fan of the Tracy and Hepburn collaborations. Certainly not in comparison to the outings of Hepburn and Cary Grant. To me, on-screen, Hepburn and Grant have a sizzle that Hepburn and Tracy just don't. But there's something contextually odd about that opinion, because in real life Hepburn and Tracy were a longtime couple, while Hepburn and Grant were not. But it just goes to further prove that real-life romance does not always translate to the viewer on-screen.

Why don't the Hepburn-Tracy comedies sit right with me? Most likely because there tends to be an inherent sexism in them. In films like *Woman of the Year* (1942) and *Adam's Rib* (1949), Hepburn plays headstrong women with thriving careers who clash with Tracy's

Tracy and Hepburn over drinks in *Woman of the Year* (1942).

characters, men who are equals to her but are somehow framed as more salt of the earth. Hepburn is taught a lesson in these movies. She can have her own ideas, but only up to a point.

In these movies there's often a late-coming power reversal in which Hepburn is humbled, which can be difficult to believe, especially given what we know about their relationship. Without Hepburn, Tracy would never have been cast in *Woman of the Year*. The script by Ring Lardner Jr. and Michael Kanin was written with Hepburn in mind, but she wanted Tracy to star opposite her. She had been a huge fan of Tracy's, according to Anne Edwards's biography *Katharine Hepburn: A Remarkable Woman*. He had never seen one of her films. But she insisted he be hired on to the movie. It was immediately obvious that there was a mutual attraction, and by the time filming wrapped up they had begun an affair. "Everyone on set realized what was happening," Edwards wrote. "The two stars had fallen quite simply and sincerely in love."

It wasn't an easy coupling, but it was a loyal one. Tracy wouldn't divorce his wife because of his dedicated Catholic beliefs. Still, once he and Hepburn were linked, they were inseparable, and she began to look for projects they could do together.

Woman of the Year cast Hepburn as a fearless war and international newspaper correspondent, while Tracy was the paper's baseball writer. He's enraged by her comments that baseball should be suspended during World War II. They form a truce, and he takes her to a game, where they start to get along. The relationship develops into a romance, and they quickly get married. And yet his frustration builds in their new domestic arrangement. Her life is fast-moving and full of worldly people who intimidate him. As the narrative progresses, she concedes that she must commit to being a wife sometimes. It's a demoralizing ending from a modern perspective. You want to see him level up to her, rather than seeing her cede her hard-won power.

Spencer Tracy smooches Katharine Hepburn in *Adam's Rib* (1949).

The 1949 title *Adam's Rib*, written by Ruth Gordon and Garson Kanin and directed by Hepburn's dear friend George Cukor, pits them in another battle of the sexes. Here they play an already married lawyer couple who find themselves on opposing sides of a case of attempted murder, in which an abused wife (Judy Holliday) tried to shoot her cheating husband. Hepburn's Amanda represents the woman, arguing that this housewife was driven to her crime by years of neglect and torment, making it a case for women's rights. Tracy's

Adam believes the law is the law. They clash in court, and she ends up winning. Is it a triumph? No. It puts a wedge in their marriage, and he feels he must prove to her that she was wrong.

To do so he accosts her while she's caught in an accidental embrace with a mutual friend who has long harbored a crush on her. Tracy threatens Hepburn with a gun before biting the barrel, revealing that it's chocolate and proving that a crime is a crime in his book. Later, during their divorce proceeding, he breaks down in tears, and they get back together—but not before he reveals that those tears were faked: Men can do emotional manipulation as well as women, he says.

Reduced to its essence, *Adam's Rib* is about a woman who wins an impressive case and then faces her husband's manipulation. It irks me to see Hepburn in these roles, and she and Tracy often seem more like sparring partners than they do lovers.

Despite this, audiences at the time loved seeing them together, and the release of *Adam's Rib* was highly anticipated as their return to comedy. *Movieland* announced: "The screen team of Katharine Hepburn and Spencer Tracy is almost a guarantee for a hit picture. If you remember their last comedy 'Woman of the Year,' you'll want to run to your nearest theater to see 'Adam's Rib.'" But some of the publicity around their union reads as odd. In a *Screenland* pictorial featuring images of the two kissing with the headline, "Katie Gets Her Man," the text begins: "Spencer Tracy never has been much of a romantic hero in his films so when he had to play a love scene with Katharine Hepburn in 'Adam's Rib' he found it hard to get started."

The article continues: "Of course, Spencer isn't averse to kissing gals, he's just camera shy. However, when he agreed to do it, the scene was hurriedly shot before the reluctant star had a chance to change his mind." It's awfully funny to read this little paragraph, given Hepburn and Tracy's real relationship, but it also speaks to a general discomfort Tracy had with romance on-screen, which I think comes through in his work. In *Pat and Mike* (1952)—which reunited the two with Kanin, Gordon, and Cukor—Tracy's a shady sports manager who recruits Hepburn's character, an athletics instructor, to become his new star. While they end up together, there's always something fatherly about his relationship with her. He's more of a coach than a lover.

So, for me, there is nothing quite like the pleasure of Hepburn-Grant pairings from about a decade earlier. In the Grant and Hepburn movies, he succumbs to her, whether that means submitting himself to her utter chaos in *Bringing Up Baby* (1938) or returning to a life he once rejected in *The Philadelphia Story* (1940). There's no strange moralizing, just giddy romance. And it's hard to say no to that.

The movies of Doris Day and Rock Hudson require even more suspension of disbelief than most modern rom-coms. The three films they made together—*Pillow Talk* (1959), *Lover Come Back* (1961), and *Send Me No Flowers* (1964)—are all particularly frothy delights with absolutely ludicrous plots. In *Pillow Talk* they war over a shared telephone line, then he attempts to trick her by posing as a naive Texan instead of the lady-killing New York songwriter he is. In *Lover Come Back* they are advertising professionals, who are yet again fighting, this time over an account. He pretends to be a nerdy scientist to win her over and throw her off from his (again) lady-killing adman. Finally, in *Send Me No Flowers* they are married, and he's an extreme hypochondriac, convinced that he's dying. He tries to set her up with a new spouse, thinking he's not long for this world. She thinks this aloofness means he's cheating on her, and everything goes haywire.

All these films seem to exist in a world that's just not quite our own. It could be because of the soundstage versions of New York where they were filmed. It could be because the scenarios are just so silly and fantastical. (In *Lover Come Back* the real scientist that Hudson is pretending to be creates a candy that's just straight alcohol,

Doris Day being quite literally whisked away by Rock Hudson in *Pillow Talk* (1959).

Rock Hudson in disguise in *Lover Come Back* (1961) alongside Doris Day.

leading to wild drunken revelry.) It could be that Day and Hudson are near-perfect avatars of standard female and male beauty of the early 1960s—her with her coiffed blonde hair and him with his tall stature and thick chest. Whatever it is, watching these movies is like entering a bubble bath. The rest of the world slips away.

But that real world complicates things. And knowing about the real personas of Day and Hudson fascinatingly colors their collaborations as well.

When Hudson was starring in these movies, he was a deeply closeted gay man. Day, meanwhile, projected a sunny exterior, but her life was filled with hardship. She had been abused by her first husband and was at the time married to someone who, according to a report in *Vanity Fair*, was "an awful man, pushy, grating on the nerves, crass." That spouse would leave her deeply in debt at the time of his death in 1968. Their lives on-screen were messy with bickering and zany situations. Off-screen, their existences were tinged with tragedy. Together they were both products of an unfair, prejudiced world.

Not that those personal details were known or relevant to audiences at the time. By 1962, Doris Day was the number-one female star in Hollywood, according to trade paper *Box Office*. She had been in second place in 1959 and 1961. Hudson was number two for 1962. Actress Angie Dickinson described Hudson's appeal in a 1964 newspaper story, calling him "devilish," and saying he can "drive you crazy at a dinner table." Born Roy Fitzgerald, Hudson was initially known for serious parts. James Wolcott wrote in *Vanity Fair*: "In his early films Rock was often photographed as a scenic landmark or natural formation." He later starred in Douglas Sirk melodramas before uniting with Day. Day, meanwhile, was a pop singer with a squeaky-clean reputation. In a 1959 column, the famous gadfly Hedda Hopper wrote: "With all the unfavorable garbage the public reads about Hollywood, Doris is one of the stars who represents the nicer things."

But you would be absolutely mistaken if you thought that somehow Day and Hudson's movies were completely retrograde, inaccessible to modern audiences. Rather than a Donna Reed–type homemaker, Day's characters—with the exception of the wife in *Send Me No Flowers*—were all career women. She had that bubbly tenor to her voice, but she was not a pushover. And Hudson played womanizing successes who thrived in the 1960s landscape because of their sex appeal. (Again, save for *Send Me No Flowers*, which is an outlier.) Though Day and Hudson always ended up together, the films also portrayed Day's characters as ambitious women with minds of their own, often thriving in male-dominated environments.

These are movies you can enjoy at face value, relishing the fact that Day and Hudson just seem to be having a great time together. Throughout most of their collaborations, their characters are mad at each other. He's self-satisfied! She's perturbed! But it's the kind of mutual frustration that is also sheer pleasure. In an interview with *People*, long after Rock Hudson's death from AIDS in 1985, Day remembered that "It didn't take long to get to know him because he was funny." She recalled that he "named me Eunice. He always had to have a name for me. There were many of them, but Eunice he liked best." That playfulness extended on camera, the affection and friendship bubbling over. Though we understand why their friendship would never have blossomed into a real-life romance, their movies are pure fantasy, and they lean into it, having a great time doing so.

It's easy to forget the first Meg Ryan and Tom Hanks collaboration. No, it wasn't *Sleepless in Seattle* (1993), the Nora Ephron movie about a lovesick reporter chasing after a widower, which would go on to gross over $126 million worldwide during its initial release. It was *Joe Versus the Volcano* (1990), a truly bizarre rom-com, written and directed by John Patrick Shanley, best known for *Moonstruck* (1987). *Joe Versus the Volcano* is a surreal work, which stars Hanks as an office drone who finds a new lease on life when he asks out a secretary played by Ryan. That is not, however, the start of a great love story. The secretary ditches him when she finds out he is dying of a supposed "brain cloud." So, alone once again, he takes up an offer to go to a fictional island and volunteer to be a human sacrifice as part of a deal with a tycoon that will make him temporarily rich. On his way, he meets two other characters portrayed by Ryan, distinguished by their accents and hair color. This is not the Ryan and Hanks audiences would come to adore. He's maybe at his most Jimmy Stewart–esque, but she's flitting between personalities: disaffected, ditzy, flirtatious. She finally lands in the role of Patricia, a more standard

Ryan-style love interest—one who happens to be captain of the boat taking Joe to a remote civilization where he is planning to die by lava.

Joe Versus the Volcano was regarded at the time as a misfire. "Not since 'Howard the Duck' has there been a big-budget comedy with feet as flat as those of 'Joe Versus the Volcano,'" Vincent Canby wrote in the New York Times. "Many gifted people contributed to it, but there's no disbelieving the grim evidence on the screen." Time has been a bit kinder to the film's reputation. It wasn't a hit, but it wasn't a disaster at the box office, at least according to Shanley, its writer-director. And the wild tone now seems adventurous—the kind of risk that is often praised rather than condemned. Plus, for true fans of the Hanks-Ryan pairing, it's an important stepping stone.

According to a 2020 interview with Shanley, Hanks pursued the part, while he auditioned several women for the multiple parts that Ryan would play, one of whom was Julia Roberts. "Then Meg Ryan came in and she was just spectacular," he said. Besides being the first movie to pair them, Joe Versus the Volcano is key to the Ryan-Hanks lore because Nora Ephron was working on the gangster comedy My Blue Heaven (1990) on the same studio lot and visited their set frequently. "She fell in love with them as a couple on that film and cast them after that," Shanley said.

When Ryan and Hanks started the press tour for Sleepless in Seattle, the lukewarm reaction to Joe Versus the Volcano was still lingering. During a press roundtable, "Someone mentioned that his previous pairing with his co-star Meg Ryan, Joe vs. the Volcano, wasn't successful," a Tampa Bay Times journalist reported, explaining that Hanks shot back with a quip. "A grin creases his angular face, partly because he feels vindicated and partly because he knows that 1990 comedy was a stinker," the text reads. He was vindicated. Sleepless in Seattle would not suffer the same fate as Joe and would etch Ryan and Hanks in cinema history, drawing comparisons to Hepburn and Tracy.

Meg Ryan and Tom Hanks finally meet up on top of the Empire State Building at the end of *Sleepless in Seattle* (1993).

Tom and Meg were rom-com leads for a neurotic era. They both bristle with a nervous edge on-screen, as if they were hovering just on the edge of a breakdown. By the time they were connected in *Joe* they had already independently proved their bona fides in the genre—Hanks with *Splash* (1984) and *Big* (1988); Ryan with the most iconic of all rom-coms, *When Harry Met Sally . . .* (1989).

When *When Harry Met Sally . . .* paired Ryan with Billy Crystal, they were an odd couple. She was a WASP princess; he was a Jewish comedian. She and Hanks are more perfectly matched. They sometimes evoke Irene Dunne and Cary Grant, her blonde regality matched with his goofy tendency for physical comedy that can turn suave when needed.

It's funny then that in *Sleepless in Seattle*, the movie that linked their names forever, they barely appear on-screen together. Ryan falls in love with Hanks before he ever knows she exists. The most interaction she has with him prior to the Empire State Building finale is via his young son, who is playing matchmaker for his sad dad. But something about their energies are aligned. Their longing feels so in tune that somehow it makes sense that these two strangers should give romance a go.

When they teamed up again five years later for 1998's *You've Got Mail*, Hollywood was capitalizing on something all too rare, a genuine movie team. In an *Entertainment Weekly* cover story upon release of *You've Got Mail*, the author began: "They've been called the Tracy and Hepburn of their time. The cutest couple on the big screen today. The most combustible combination of chemicals to hit Hollywood's periodic table in decades. And here they are—Tom Hanks and Meg Ryan—sitting at a sidewalk cafe on Manhattan's Upper West Side, sipping ice water and doodling with their silverware as they wait to shoot a scene for *You've Got Mail*, their latest boy-almost-doesn't-meet-girl romantic comedy."

And yet both apparently had concerns about the project. Hanks was tired of the Jimmy Stewart comparisons, but this film meant taking on a version of one of Stewart's old roles, because it was a remake of Ernst Lubitsch's *The Shop Around the Corner* (1940). Ryan didn't want to be known for *only* rom-coms—and, in all fairness, she may have been right to be concerned. Ultimately, however, they both knew it was an opportunity too good to pass up.

Once again, *You've Got Mail* keeps their characters at a distance for most of the movie. They play retail rivals. He's the capitalist with the big bad chain bookstore; she has her intimate little shop where she hosts story hours and knows her customers by name. They become friends first over instant messenger, anonymously sharing their hopes and fears, before he ultimately realizes that the person he has been communicating with is the same person who has been antagonizing him in public life. As the plot nears its end, they have become actual friends, though he keeps the secret of his online alter ego until the final moment. In Riverside Park, he reveals that he was her digital pen pal all along. She replies that she was hoping it was him.

Why do Meg and Tom work even—or maybe mostly—when they are apart? I think it's because you can feel their brains whirring. Both are, of course, extremely attractive people, and yet it's their intellectual connection that drives their most successful work. (This also might be why there was never really any serious speculation as to whether they were an actual couple.) Even though she's basically a stalker in one, and in the other they are enemies, through Ephron's writing and their collective interpretation of that wit, we are convinced that they are ideal for each other. Tom and Meg just fit—even if they are never in the same room.

One might not immediately think of Adam Sandler as a rom-com star. The Sandman is arguably best known for his over-the-top comedies, where romance is secondary to the antics. But somehow, along the way, he established his own rom-com industry. In the movies that built the Sandler brand, his love interests are often blonde and slightly bland. There's the kindly schoolteacher in *Billy Madison* (1995), played by Bridgette Wilson, and the nice golf publicist in *Happy Gilmore* (1996), played by Julie Bowen. In *Big Daddy* (1999), Joey Lauren Adams puts a sort of edgy spin on this type, but she's ultimately a spectator to his nonsense.

That's why it was a revelation when Sandler was paired for the first time with Drew Barrymore in 1998's *The Wedding Singer*. The 1980s-set movie is about wedding singer Robbie Hart, played by Sandler, who falls for Julia Sullivan, a waitress at the reception hall where he works, played by Barrymore. Julia is set to marry a cocky dude, but it's obvious that she is charmed by Robbie, his mullet, and his

Drew Barrymore and Adam Sandler in *The Wedding Singer* (1998).

aggressive-sweet entertainment style. He's an off-kilter guy and she's not so straitlaced herself. She's genuine but not cookie cutter, and though it's not explicitly written, she has the classic quirk that Drew Barrymore brings to every role. That's the great match of Sandler and Barrymore: two weirdos who fizz when they are on-screen together.

When *The Wedding Singer* came out, Barrymore and Sandler were at vastly different points in their careers. Sandler was on a hot streak—his breakout time on *Saturday Night Live* had translated into movie stardom, thanks to *Madison* and *Gilmore*. Barrymore, meanwhile, was in a period of career rebuild. She became a star when she was seven years old in *E.T. the Extra-Terrestrial* (1982) but struggled publicly off-screen. When she returned to stardom, she began playing teens gone bad in the likes of erotic thriller *Poison Ivy* (1992), but by 1998 she was crafting a different kind of image. Not only did she star as Julia in *The Wedding Singer*, but she also turned herself into a modern interpretation of Cinderella in *Ever After* (1998). Suddenly, Drew could be an American Sweetheart again after her time as a rebel.

Still, in a newspaper story about *The Wedding Singer* at the time of its release, a writer mused: "Do these two radically different actors strike you as a likely hot screen couple in a romantic comedy?" Now, the answer is obvious. Then, it seemed like a long shot. But what worked was their clear affection for each other. In that same article, Sandler described Barrymore as "like when the DJ keeps playing songs you like. Every time she starts up a story—'Wow! I like the story.' She's a sweetheart." The project came to fruition because they just wanted to work together: Sandler's *SNL* buddies had the idea and Barrymore had her production company, Flower Films.

By the time they appeared together again six years later in *50 First Dates* (2004), their reunion was celebrated as the next great coming of the rom-com couple. *50 First Dates*—which is set in Hawaii because it's where Barrymore and Sandler went on a vacation after filming *The Wedding Singer*—leans harder into the zaniness of Barrymore and Sandler's respective personalities. He plays a marine biologist who deals with vomiting sea mammals and woos women who come to Hawaii for vacation and leave. But then he becomes fascinated with a girl he meets at a local diner. In their meet-cute, he helps her build a structure out of her waffles. But, alas, there's a problem. Turns out she was in a car accident that causes her to wake up thinking it's the morning of her traumatic incident every single day. The ruse is kept up by her loving father and brother, who don't really think through the implications of what they are doing. But Sandler's love starts to challenge that.

50 First Dates features an unusual mix of tones. On the one hand, Drew's character's impediment makes everything seem very, well, sad. But it's mixed with gross Sandler gags and Rob Schneider running around doing an offensive accent. At the same time, it's hard not to buy into their coupling, because they are seemingly on the same wavelength.

Post–*Wedding Singer*, Barrymore embraced her silliness. In her rom-com *Never Been Kissed* (1999), in which she plays a reporter who goes undercover as a high school student, she embraced her dorkiness as the nerdy "Josie Grossie" in flashbacks. In time, Barrymore has only gotten wackier.

It all makes sense that she and Sandler would be simpatico, and when you watch them together in *50 First Dates* you feel the buzz of their collective goofiness—Sandler's love for funny voices and disgusting moments makes him an ideal partner for Barrymore's own barely buried quirk.

THE BAXTER, THE BAD GIRL, AND THE BEST FRIEND

THE ROM-COM ECOSYSTEM IS MADE UP OF MORE THAN JUST the two lovers at the center of the story. There is also the cast of characters who orbit them, either providing emotional support or acting as barriers to happiness. A rom-com does not need to have these figures, but they frequently appear in different permutations. As with any film that indulges in a trope, the best ones complicate and deepen what could be surface-level descriptions. At the same time, these are easily identifiable people in the rom-com universe, and they go by certain names. The Best Friend, the Bad Girl, and the Baxter.

First, the Best Friend. The Best Friend can be of any gender, but their main role is to aid and abet our hero or heroine. They may have their own plotlines, but their travails are secondary to what the protagonist is going through. Any issues they may have are easily resolved. If a woman is Best Friends with a female character, she

OPPOSITE: Ralph Bellamy in *His Girl Friday* (1940).

Tony Randall offers Rock Hudson a light in *Pillow Talk* (1959).

is usually framed as slightly less attractive or at least less desirable than her counterpart. There's no way this woman would draw away the focus from the lead. Instead, she's there to provide some sort of comic relief.

Then: The Bad Girl. The Bad Girl is the opposition. Her raison d'être is to cause problems for our main squeeze, and she always gets cast aside at the end. She's a menace, and often a brunette, particularly if our heroine is blonde.

Finally: The Baxter. The Baxter is defined as such by the 2005 movie *The Baxter*, starring Michael Showalter, as a character who identifies as a "Baxter." Basically, this is the guy who gets left at the altar when the better option (our hero, typically) comes along. He's a nice dude, and you feel a little bad for him, but not quite bad enough that you care about his probably deeply broken heart.

The Best Friend, the Bad Girl, and the Baxter have origins in the screwball days, particularly the Baxter. But they also all gained a stronger foothold in the modern era of rom-coms, when the genre became more standardized. The Best Friend, as well, particularly exploded in the 1980s through the 2000s, when women's inner lives were of more interest to general audiences than they were in the Hays Code era. Before, women frequently had only employees or relatives to confide in. Sometimes they had no one: They were lone wolves in men's worlds. Eventually, they got their own pals.

Which isn't to say that the Best Friend cannot be male. In fact, the male Best Friend arguably predated the female one. Look at Eddie Albert in *Roman Holiday* (1953), playing Irving Radovich, the photographer to Gregory Peck's Joe Bradley. Irving is Joe's partner in crime, secretly taking photos of Audrey Hepburn's Princess Ann without her knowledge. He's a little crasser than Joe and is willing to humiliate himself for a shot. Irving holds no candle, however, to the king of the male Best Friend: essentially, any character played by Tony Randall in the Doris Day–Rock Hudson movies.

While Hudson portrayed alpha male playboys, Randall played squirrely, uptight, and anxious men. They were usually of a higher economic status than Hudson's paragons of machismo, but more easily dismissed, more willing to get involved and frazzled in their peer's schemes. In *Pillow Talk* (1959) he's Jonathan Forbes, a millionaire who happens to be both a client of Day's interior decorator and a pal-slash-benefactor of Hudson's composer. Jonathan is enamored of Day's Jan, but she rejects his advances with cute pity rather than something to be taken seriously. Meanwhile, in *Lover Come Back* (1961) he's the boss at the ad agency where Hudson's character works, constantly in over his head thanks to Hudson's wacky ways of getting clients.

The unspoken subtext that complicates matters is the idea that Randall's characters frequently read as possibly being gay. The assumption was even verbalized in *Down with Love*, the 2003 parody of the Day-Hudson romps that featured David Hyde Pierce in the Randall role. With changing social mores, Gay Best Friend did emerge as a trope to be both indulged and subverted. *My Best Friend's Wedding* (1997) had Rupert Everett as the gay pal for Julia Roberts, a boisterous presence who is responsible for leading a wedding party in an "I Say a Little Prayer" sing-along. Everett's presence was so welcome that his role was increased in the process of making the film. But the Gay Best Friend became so much of a trope that rom-coms in the 2010s began to subvert it. In 2011's *Friends with Benefits*, Woody Harrelson, in full bro mode, plays the Best Friend of Justin Timberlake's magazine art director. He wears basketball shorts and seems like your typical guy, but he's also—surprise—gay! He's a dude who loves other dudes. It's a subversion that perpetuates the inaccurate stereotype that it's shocking for a gay man to be masculine in this manner. The film *Set It Up* (2018) does something similar, casting *Saturday Night Live* star Pete Davidson as the Gay Best Friend of the lead. Davidson and Harrelson are playing their roles the same way they would if their characters were straight,

Bruno Kirby and Carrie Fisher as Jess and Marie counsel the main characters in *When Harry Met Sally . . .* (1989).

but the fact that they are gay is a way for the filmmakers to show how progressive they are—and how progressive their male leads are.

Has the Best Friend—male or female—ever been done perfectly? Yes. As previously established, there's a reason Nora Ephron and Rob Reiner's *When Harry Met Sally . . .* is so revered, and, sure, it has a lot to do with the witty dialogue and chemistry between Meg Ryan and Billy Crystal. But I would venture to say it is also because of Jess

(Bruno Kirby) and Marie (Carrie Fisher). At the outset of the plot, Jess is Harry's friend who listens to him whine about his ex at baseball games; Marie is part of Sally's coterie and maintains a Rolodex of potential dates, thinking of men as a business she must participate in. Harry and Sally, after becoming friends, try to set up the other with Jess and Marie, who over dinner quickly fall for one another after Marie quotes Jess's own writing back to him. (Never forget: "Pesto is the quiche of the eighties.")

Marie and Jess go home together, both making up a ruse to get in the same cab, and in the blink of an eye, they are in a relationship. It's not without friction. They fight as any couple would over decorating their apartment. He wants his wagon-wheel coffee table prominently displayed; she thinks it is hideous. But their romance also feels easy

Judy Greer schemes as an evil Best Friend in *13 Going on 30* (2004) alongside Jennifer Garner.

and lived in. They take comfort in the certainty of their coupling, while Harry and Sally get into more lasting scrapes because they refuse to be honest with each other. In their team-like camaraderie Marie and Jess are an example of what Harry and Sally could be: good friends who also happen to be lovers.

They are also more than just sidekicks. In their own romance they are fully realized human beings living in tandem with the heroes, rather than just supporting them along their journey. All Best Friends should aspire to be Jess and Marie, who maybe have the most aspirational love story of the entire movie.

There is a Holy Trinity of actresses who excel in the Best Friend department: Joan Cusack, Judy Greer, and Kathryn Hahn.

Greer is arguably the most famous Best Friend in rom-com history, even if sometimes the characters she plays aren't even really Best Friends, but other forms of supporting players. She's appeared in *The Wedding Planner* (2001), *What Women Want* (2000), *Elizabethtown* (2005), and *27 Dresses* (2008). Even her memoir jokes about her character-actor status with the title *I Don't Know What You Know Me From: My Life as a Co-Star*.

For years, fans have crowed that to reduce Greer to where her credits fall on the call sheet doesn't account for the praise she actually deserves. And, indeed, Greer's BFF characters can have layers. In *13 Going on 30* (2004), for instance, Lucy Wyman at first seems like she'd be content to fade into the background, but she turns out to have her own conniving intentions to steal heroine Jenna Rink's job and ruin her life. She's a Best Friend with Bad Girl flavoring. This is not entirely uncommon: On the flip side of that trend there's Selma Blair's Vivian Kensington in *Legally Blonde* (2001), who starts out as an antagonist to Reese Witherspoon's Elle Woods, mocking her and dating her ex. Vivian eventually becomes Elle's Best Friend when she realizes that the man in question is a total dolt.

Melanie Griffith and Joan Cusack rock huge hair in *Working Girl* (1988).

Still, it's Greer's essential kookiness—her high-pitched voice and ability to play just slightly off-kilter—that has allowed her to thrive in this arena. Kathryn Hahn displays similar energy in 2003's *How to Lose a Guy in 10 Days*. Her character is the emotional disaster who inspires Kate Hudson's put-together Andie to do an experiment based on her failings. She's introduced crying over a guy she's only dated for a week, while wearing a hideous nightgown with a frilly collar. And Hahn's physicality has a clear antecedent in Joan Cusack, a mother figure of these kinds of BFFs.

Take Cusack in 1988's *Working Girl*, in which she plays Cyn. Melanie Griffiths's heroine Tess McGill is from Staten Island, starting out with big hair and a bit of a flashy sense of style. But Cyn is the embodiment of the stereotype of that borough. Her hair is big, her accent is thick, and her dresses have as many bows as possible. When Tess is doing chores for her patrician boss Katharine Parker (Sigourney Weaver), it's Cyn who encourages her to try on Katharine's fancy clothes. After Tess gets nervous, Cyn accidentally slips her a few too many Valiums, which leads to light intoxication rather than dangerous incapacitation. (The beauty of the rom-com!) Cyn is cheeky, but she poses absolutely no threat to Tess. She can ask Harrison Ford's Jack Trainer if he wants "Coffee? Tea? Me?" and no one would seriously believe that he would even consider the third option.

Working Girl also happens to include one of rom-coms' most famous Bad Girls: Weaver's Katharine Parker. Katharine is initially introduced as what Tess aspires to be. She's a stylish, competent businesswoman, staking her place in 1980s Wall Street—a universe that is dominated by men. She at first appears to be mentoring Tess, offering her advice, saying she'll push her ideas through.

Then she goes on a skiing vacation, hurts herself, and starts using Tess less as a business assistant and more as a maid. Tess realizes that Katharine is never going to help her accomplish her proposed project, so she takes matters into her own hands and meets and collaborates with Jack, who, it turns out, is Katharine's boyfriend. While Tess is the one who ends up sleeping with Katharine's partner behind her back, you never really feel *all* that bad for her because Katharine's such a monster—a ruthless striver who steals Tess's prized intellectual property.

And Weaver's performance gives you every reason to hate Katharine. She plays her with an elegant flair that nevertheless oozes with snobby superiority. You get the sense that she got where she is not because she was qualified but because she knew the right people.

There are other Bad Girls who aren't quite as nasty as Katharine, just deluded figures with a whiff of cruelty to them. A fine example of this is Melissa De Sousa's Shelby in *The Best Man* (1999) and its sequel *The Best Man Holiday* (2013). Shelby is technically part of the core group of friends who make up the plot of the ensemble rom-com, but the rest of them all seem to hate her because she is vain and puts down the women around her. She emasculates and controls her boyfriend Julian (Harold Perrineau) who ends up finding love with Candy (Regina Hall), a stripper with a heart of gold. The sequel, *The Best Man Holiday*, gives Shelby some more layers, even though she has become a cast member on *Real Housewives* and conspires to end Julian and Candy's marriage. She's thoroughly entertaining, but you also know it would be better for Julian to leave her behind.

Similarly, you can point to Parker Posey's hilarious Patricia Eden in *You've Got Mail* (1998) as another example of the Bad Girl. A powerful book editor, Patricia is smart and accomplished but has a capitalist edge that Meg Ryan's Kathleen Kelly lacks. She's not mean so much as uncaring. When she and Hanks's Joe Fox get stuck in an elevator her main concern is finding her Tic Tacs—not contemplating their precarious situation with an existential spiral. She promises that if she ever gets out, she's getting her eyes lasered. Ultimately, she's just not the right person for Joe, even though on paper they seem perfectly suited.

And this is where the Bad Girl and the Baxter start to overlap. The Bad Girl in many ways is just a Baxter by a different name, but that difference shows the inherent sexism that these titles carry. The woman the man leaves behind on the way to his one true love deserves to be rejected. Meanwhile the Baxter, the man who gets dropped for the other guy, gets pity. Sure, there are occasionally Bastards—male spins on the Bad Girls—who get dumped. In *The Wedding Singer* (1998), Drew Barrymore's character is engaged to an awful bro, who is cleary the wrong guy. But generally the Baxter is just too nice, while the Bad Girl is just too mean.

Ralph Bellamy stuck in the middle of Cary Grant and Rosalind Russell in *His Girl Friday* (1940).

Michael Showalter may have coined the term "the Baxter" in the film of the same name, but he was drawing on a long history of these types of guys.

The spiritual father of them all is Ralph Bellamy. In fact, if you ignore "the Baxter" you can use Bellamy's name as a stand-in for this type of guy entirely, as Billy Mernit does in his book *Writing the Romantic Comedy*. Mernit defines *the Bellamy* as the "Other Man or Woman, the Wrong Guy or Girl." He adds that Bellamy was "presentable enough in terms of social status, he was neither deep in temperament nor desirable in appearance and he was usually saddled with a profession that screamed boredom."

Bellamy's career didn't start this way. In a 1936 issue of *Picturegoer*, he was described as "one of the most popular of the 'he-man' lovers." So while Bellamy was no slouch in the romantic-lead department, he crumbled when you made him an alternative to Cary Grant. The key Bellamy films are *The Awful Truth* (1937) and *His Girl Friday* (1940), both of which present him as the somewhat doltish alternative to Cary Grant's swaggering main love interest.

In other circumstances, Bellamy's characters might be the right choice for the female leads. In both *His Girl Friday* and *The Awful Truth* the women in question—Rosalind Russell and Irene Dunne, respectively—are running away from the tumultuous relationships they have with Grant's men. Russell's Hildy Johnson wants out of the news business and to start a quiet life with Bellamy's insurance salesman instead of the chaotic working relationship she has with her ex. Dunne and Grant's couple in *The Awful Truth* have gotten divorced and now she's with Bellamy, an ingratiating oilman who might be a bit of a Bastard in his quest for wealth. But both Dunne and Russell ultimately realize that they want the excitement of a Grant in their lives. Bellamy's just too boring and too dorky.

That's the thing with the Baxter; he's just sort of bland. One of my personal favorite Baxters is played by Danny Aiello in *Moonstruck* (1987). When the film opens, Cher's Loretta Castorini is dating Aiello's Johnny Cammareri. Here's how we know he's wrong for her. In one of the very first scenes, he asks her to marry him, but he does so in a way that is so completely unromantic that she forces him to redo his proposal and get down on one knee. Then she says yes, but there's a sense of obligation to their relationship. Johnny isn't just less attractive than Ronny, his younger brother who Loretta ultimately gets together with, he's sort of a dolt. He always leaves his suitcase behind. He is so dedicated to his mother that he hangs on her every word.

Loretta is settling and she knows it and we know it. That's what the Baxter represents: a version of a less exciting life.

Other than Bellamy, the actor most associated with the Baxter is Bill Pullman, who embodies the type in *Sleepless in Seattle* (1993) as Walter. Showalter explained in an interview at the time of *The Baxter*'s release that it was Walter who served as the main inspiration. "I think the Bill Pullman character in that is really a great character. He's really funny and I love all of his scenes in it. Then about halfway through the movie, she dumps him. Then it becomes about her and Tom Hanks and I didn't identify as well with Tom Hanks, who is just kind of perfect in every way."

In *Sleepless*, Walter and Meg Ryan's Annie are engaged to be married and she even finds him perfectly enjoyable to spend time around. But he's just not sexy. He's got allergies and his name, Walter, is even unexciting. Annie is far more intrigued by the lovelorn man she hears on the radio, talking about his dead wife. Poor Bill Pullman isn't even interesting enough to compete with a guy she's never met. When Annie requests to go meet her mystery man on the top of the Empire State Building, Walter simply acquiesces. It really shouldn't be as easy as it is to let him go.

Two years later Pullman was able to get his revenge in *While You Were Sleeping* (1995). That rom-com casts him as a man who would otherwise be a Baxter. He's the brother of the handsome comatose patient (Peter Gallagher) whom Sandra Bullock's ticket taker on the Chicago L, Lucy, is in love with from afar. When Lucy's crush finally wakes up, you would expect Pullman, being who he is as an actor, to be cast aside, but he ultimately wins Lucy's affections. And she leaves Gallagher's character Peter at the altar. For once, the Baxter triumphs. Or maybe Peter, as handsome as he is, was the Baxter all along. Especially since he's not really the guy of her dreams anyway.

This is also the concept of *The Baxter*, which is told from the perspective of a man, Elliot Sherman (Showalter), who self-identifies as

Michael Showalter, also the director, embodies the idea of "the Baxter" in *The Baxter* (2005) alongside Michelle Williams.

this type. Elliot has all the hallmarks. He's an accountant (boring) who lives in Brooklyn (at that time, not very chic) and reads the dictionary for fun. He's sweet but he has a problem: All his girlfriends end up falling for someone else, mostly men they once knew who, almost as if by magic, reemerge. Elliot gets engaged to a gorgeous, vivacious girl, Caroline Swann (Elizabeth Banks) and is seemingly headed toward more Baxterdom when her suave high school ex, Bradley Lake (Justin Theroux), suddenly reappears. Except there's another girl waiting for him in the wings, Cecil Mills (Michelle Williams), the person he should have been with all along. *The Baxter* is at once a deconstruction of rom-coms while also a rom-com itself. Caroline becomes something of the archetypal Bad Girl and Cecil is a classically quirky heroine in the body of a female Baxter. Elliot has his own gang of goofy pals, the

Best Friends of the Baxter, who at this point is the romantic lead. (Can you keep it all straight?)

The Baxter proves, more than anything, that to try to parody a rom-com will likely lead to a vicious cycle. Try to play with the tropes as much as you want and it's more than likely you are making a love letter to exactly the kinds of things a rom-com always does.

It's the beauty of the rom-com, stock characters included: Do it right and it's infallible.

THE HIGH-MAINTENANCE WOMAN

"OOOH, INGRID BERGMAN, NOW SHE'S LOW-MAINTENANCE."

Harry Burns and Sally Albright are each watching *Casablanca* when Harry says this to Sally over the phone.

"Low-maintenance?" Sally asks.

"There are two kinds of women: high-maintenance and low-maintenance," he explains.

Sally asks which one she is.

"You're the worst kind," he responds. "You're high-maintenance, but you think you're low-maintenance."

Signs of Sally's "high-maintenance" behavior were already sprinkled throughout *When Harry Met Sally...* (1989) before this conversation. When she orders food at restaurants, it's a whole production. To paraphrase her dialogue, she wants apple pie à la mode, but she wants the pie heated and she wants the ice cream on the side, not on top. It should be strawberry, not vanilla, and if they don't have strawberry,

OPPOSITE: Meg Ryan in *When Harry Met Sally...* (1989).

she doesn't want ice cream and she doesn't want the pie heated. Harry, on the other hand, just orders a "number three."

Of course, Harry ultimately decides he loves her for the very qualities that make her high-maintenance. They all come out in his dramatic confession on New Year's Eve that ends the movie, in which he says that he loves that it takes her an hour and a half to order a sandwich.

But if Nora Ephron verbalized the idea of the high-maintenance rom-com heroine in *When Harry Met Sally . . .* she certainly did not invent it. It's an archetype that has spread throughout the history of the genre and has been exemplified by women ranging from Katharine Hepburn to Doris Day to Lucy Liu. These characters often have rules they follow. Jean Arthur has a strict morning routine in *The More the Merrier* (1943). In *Something New* (2006), Sanaa Lathan has a long list of dislikes, and an even longer list of what she requires in a man. Even Ingrid Bergman has played a high-maintenance woman, specifically in *Cactus Flower* (1969), where she's a diligent nurse.

Like many rom-com tropes, it's a tricky thing. The high-maintenance heroine is often someone to admire. She's self-possessed and good at her job. She knows what she wants. She's smart. So where's the problem? Sometimes the movies imply that she somehow needs to be fixed, whatever that means. That tough exterior needs to be softened a little and her haughty demeanor needs to be corrected. Ephron had her male hero love her high-maintenance woman because Ephron herself was a high-maintenance woman, but history has not always been as kind to those who fit the description.

If there's a star who exemplifies the high-maintenance trope, it's Katharine Hepburn. No other screen star quite projected her untouchable aura. In *The Philadelphia Story* (1940), George, the husband-to-be of her character Tracy Lord, describes her as "some marvelous, distant, well, queen" and like a "statue." This bothers Tracy, who wants to be regarded as, frankly, a human being rather than something to be admired, and yet it also does a good job of summing up what Hepburn represented on-screen. Just look at her: She's imperiousness incarnate, tall and broad-shouldered with *that* voice and its thick timber.

Throughout *The Philadelphia Story*, Tracy tries to break free from the confines of George's impressions of her. She gets drunk and goes swimming, and eventually falls back in love with her ex, C. K. Dexter Haven, played by Cary Grant. But maybe the best example of Hepburn's "high-maintenance" woman came two years later in *Woman of the Year* (1942), the first movie in which she appeared opposite Spencer Tracy. Her character, Tess Harding, is a fantastically accomplished newspaperwoman, both a savvy war correspondent as well as the toast of New York society, who finds herself surprisingly smitten with a surly sports reporter.

Watching *Woman of the Year* in the twenty-first century, you're at first struck by just how titanic Tess is as a character and Hepburn is as an actress. At the same time, there's a sinking dread that Tess will somehow reform, and that is the case, albeit in a strange way. In the finale, Tess tries to win over Spencer's character, Sam, by attempting domesticity. She fumbles her way through making breakfast for him, resulting in disaster. It's a bravura sequence of physical comedy for Hepburn as she wrestles with the toaster and the coffee maker, but it's also a bit depressing. And Hepburn reportedly felt that way too.

Hepburn had shepherded *Woman of the Year* into existence on the basis of her own star power. The idea for the film came from writer Garson Kanin, who based it on the journalist Dorothy Thompson, with Hepburn in mind for the lead role. Hepburn loved the idea and brought it to Metro-Goldwyn-Mayer, demanded that Tracy star opposite her, and finagled a way to get the writers—Kanin, his brother Mike, and Ring Lardner Jr.—paid far more than they otherwise would have, a show of her influence within the studio system. But even Hepburn was reportedly angry at the way the movie ended.

Katharine Hepburn in her finery as Tess in *Woman of the Year* (1942).

According to Hepburn's biographer, Anne Edwards, the original
plan was for Tess to accompany Sam to a baseball game, a sign of
respect for his industry as much as hers. But Stevens and producer
Joseph L. Mankiewicz were reportedly worried that the average American woman would be put off by Tess and all her professional success, so a new ending was crafted in which Tess was humiliated for
the sake of her husband. Kate, apparently, called it "the worst bunch
of shit I've read." But the intended effect worked. Bosley Crowther,
writing in the *New York Times*, noted that "A picture more carefully
designed to stimulate the emotions and flatter the egos of the average
American citizen, man or woman, has seldom been made."

It's an ending that feels entirely counter to the character with
whom the audience just spent time, as well as the entire ethos of Hepburn's stardom.

Doris Day never really gave off the high-maintenance vibes the same
way that Hepburn did. In the pantheon of stars, she was approachable,
a pop singer turned movie star with a sunny disposition. When she
died, she was called "America's archetypal girl next door." And yet in
her first two collaborations with Rock Hudson, she fully fits the mold of
the woman whose ambition needs to be reined in by Hudson's playboy.

Day's own persona was a mass of contradictions. She was at the
same time "chaste" and embroiled in these overtly sexual scenarios.
She was seen as a safe celebrity, while often playing women who
were at the top of their fields. The tagline for *Pillow Talk* (1959) was:
"The captivating story of what happens when . . . A carefree bachelor
who believes in 'togetherness' tangles with a carefree career girl who
insists on 'singleness'!!!!" But how "carefree" were these Day characters really? Jan Morrow in *Pillow Talk* is an interior decorator whose
job is all about the maintenance of space. She is first angry at Hudson's Brad Allen because his antics with other women on their shared
party line drive her nuts. His life is messy. Her life is clean. In the end,

he quite literally abducts her from her bed and carries her into his apartment.

Thanks to their aligned star power, Day and Hudson make this palatable, where others might have failed. Just three years after *Lover Come Back* (1961), Natalie Wood and Tony Curtis starred in *Sex and the Single Girl* (1964), a very loose adaptation of Helen Gurley Brown's groundbreaking book of advice for young women. Wood is the author, a psychologist who happens to be a virgin despite her book about intercourse, and Curtis is the lad mag editor trying to expose her by getting her in the sack. Unlike the Day and Hudson comedies, you never really believe the chemistry between Wood and Curtis. Wood eventually gives in, abandoning her ideals—based on her years of research—for a man. The notion that an educated, accomplished woman should be choosy about whom she sleeps with is thrown out the window.

The high-maintenance woman, as embodied by Meg Ryan in *When Harry Met Sally . . .* and other Nora Ephron–penned rom-coms, owes a lot to Doris Day. A Ryan character is a lot like a Day character. Blonde, yes, but also highly intelligent, prickly at times, and, above all, likable. They are proud of the lives they've built and don't take kindly to people—specifically, men—interrupting those lives. Except, of course, when romance gets the better of them.

But Sally's high-maintenance qualities are rendered lovingly. Why? Because her traits were written by a high-maintenance woman.

Even before her untimely death, Nora Ephron's own peculiarities were mythologized, mostly by herself. Like Sally, she had very specific opinions on food and when and how to eat it. (She once told Maureen Dowd in a *New York Times* column that she convinced a 20th Century Fox executive to let her direct her own movie because she told him exactly what to order at the Russian Tea Room in New York. It was the cabbage borscht and it was "delicious.")

Katherine Heigl faces the prospect of motherhood alongside Seth Rogen in *Knocked Up* (2007).

For Ephron's heroines, being high-maintenance was not something they had to overcome. It's just who they were, and the men around them appreciated that. Maybe not immediately, of course. In *When Harry Met Sally . . .,* Harry is initially befuddled by Sally's eccentricities, but as soon as they become friends, he learns not only to live with them, but to love them. One might say that in *You've Got Mail* (1998), Ryan's Kathleen Kelly ultimately seduces Tom Hanks's Joe Fox with her romanticized high-maintenance qualities—talk of smelling pencils and frustration with Starbucks and love of Jane Austen. When they meet in person, he's not repulsed because she's particular; he just realizes that she is his enemy in business.

Ephron was quite familiar with rom-com history. Her parents, Henry and Phoebe Ephron, were screenwriters responsible for one of Hepburn's highly capable women: the librarian in *Desk Set* (1957). So while Ephron was very distinctly paying homage to all these difficult women who came before her heroines, she was also remaking them in her own image.

Not that she hasn't received criticism for putting a name to a kind of cinematic heroine that existed long before she did. Writing for *The Atlantic* in 2019, the critic Megan Garber condemned the high-maintenance trope. She wrote: "It serves as an indictment of women who want. It neatly captures the absurdity of a culture that in one breath demands women do everything they can to 'maintain' themselves and, in the next, mocks them for making the effort." Ephron herself obviously loved the act of "maintaining"; she even once wrote a detailed essay about her own maintenance in her book *I Feel Bad About My Neck*, describing all the treatments she gets to keep up her looks. Still, Garber's point stands, and the high-maintenance woman has kept reappearing in rom-coms in ways that maybe Ephron did not intend.

Judd Apatow's rom-coms, for instance, are full of high-maintenance women whose general air of being put together is framed in contrast to the disastrous men who are trying to woo them. *Knocked Up* (2007) is perhaps the most salient and controversial example of this.

Katherine Heigl plays Alison, an ambitious E! News reporter who gets drunk one night after getting a promotion and has a one-night stand with Ben, a stoner portrayed by Seth Rogen. Through a series of miscommunications, she becomes pregnant, decides to raise the baby, and now must deal with the adult baby who is the father. Rogen gets to play the fun-loving buffoon while Heigl is forced to lay down the law. The movie does understand that Rogen's character is the one who needs to change, and yet there's still an imbalance, simply because his perspective is, well, the more fun one. Heigl famously called the movie "a little sexist" in an interview with *Vanity Fair*. She said: "It paints the women as shrews, as humorless and uptight, and it paints the men as lovable, goofy, fun-loving guys." She wasn't wrong, and it's not as if Alison was the last of her kind even as the genre has tried to evolve. As recently as 2018, *Set It Up* brought us Lucy Liu as a boss so demanding that her beleaguered assistant tries to get her a boyfriend just so she'll be less of a nightmare to work for. At least, in that case, the man she's being set up with is just as high-strung, and the movie also includes a parallel creature: the Gigantic Mess in the form of Zoey Deutch's underling, who is the kind of girl who will drunkenly eat pizza on the floor and let her mouth get covered in grease.

The Gigantic Mess doesn't care about her food order. She'll eat anything. She isn't fussy about the men (or women) she gets involved with. She's beyond low-maintenance: She just doesn't care. Amy Schumer plays one in 2015's *Trainwreck*, also directed by Judd Apatow, because she has chaotic one-night stands. Jenny Slate is one in *Obvious Child* (2014) because she's unafraid of public urination.

The Manic Pixie Dream Girl is a type of character that exists as a subgenre of the Gigantic Mess. The term, coined by the pop culture journalist Nathan Rabin, was used to describe Kirsten Dunst's character in *Elizabethtown* (2005), but more largely describes the kind

Renée Zellweger as Bridget Jones, wallowing.

of carefree gal who only exists in the heads of male writers. Natalie Portman embodied this in the Zach Braff movie *Garden State* (2004), playing a young woman who has the right taste in music and is weird—unafraid to contort herself into odd shapes with the idea of being totally original. But she's also in a state of regression, living at home with her mother, who is overprotective due to her epilepsy. You see, the Gigantic Mess may not need to be fixed in the way that the high-maintenance woman does, but she does need to be saved from herself.

If there is a patron saint of the Gigantic Mess, it is Bridget Jones in *Bridget Jones's Diary* (2001), adapted into a movie from Helen Fielding's bestseller, and directed by Sharon Maguire. Sally Albright (in *When Harry Met Sally . . .*) perfectly maintains every aspect of her existence. Bridget Jones lets herself fall into disarray. She smokes too much and drinks too much and is not stick-thin—even if her heaviness is overexaggerated in that frustratingly Hollywood way. She wears thick foundation garments to hide her tiny belly and sings to herself in her room. She has an affair with her sexy boss (Hugh Grant), who treats her like dirt. The man she ultimately ends up with, Mark Darcy (Colin Firth)—a remix of Mr. Darcy from Jane Austen's *Pride and Prejudice*—is initially turned off by Bridget's casualness and the fact that she always seems to be putting her foot in her mouth. It turns out, however, that opposites attract.

Bridget certainly wasn't the first mess in rom-com history. She carries a bit of the screwball heroine in her—the wild woman who coaxes a man out of his humdrum life. But arriving in 2001, she felt fully fresh, a counter to all the high-maintenance gals who had the genre in a chokehold for years, thanks to Sally and her ilk. And it's true, there is room for both the high-maintenance lady and the Gigantic Mess.

PERFECT ROM-COM MOMENT
BORN YESTERDAY (1950)

Intellectual exchange can be very sexy. That's the case in George Cukor's *Born Yesterday*, in which a journalist, Paul (William Holden), is hired to help a mob boss's showgirl girlfriend, Billie (Judy Holliday), appear presentable to the bigwigs of D.C. Billie is a queen of malapropisms, who has never really been encouraged to explore the world beyond her small, unstimulating universe, and Paul's a man who has always relied on his smarts and his understanding of what's right. But, of course, they teach each other some things.

This all comes to fruition when he takes her on a tour of the sights in the nation's capital and they discuss an article he has written. He's charmed when she puts on her thick glasses to go over what she doesn't understand about it, but soon he realizes that she makes great points. It's not just that his piece is full of words that she doesn't know; it's full of language that is not accessible to most Americans. If he wants to write about democracy, he should speak to the everyman—or -woman, that is. Her savviness just takes a different form from his and that's incredibly attractive.

Judy Holliday and William Holden take a tour of the capital in *Born Yesterday* (1950).

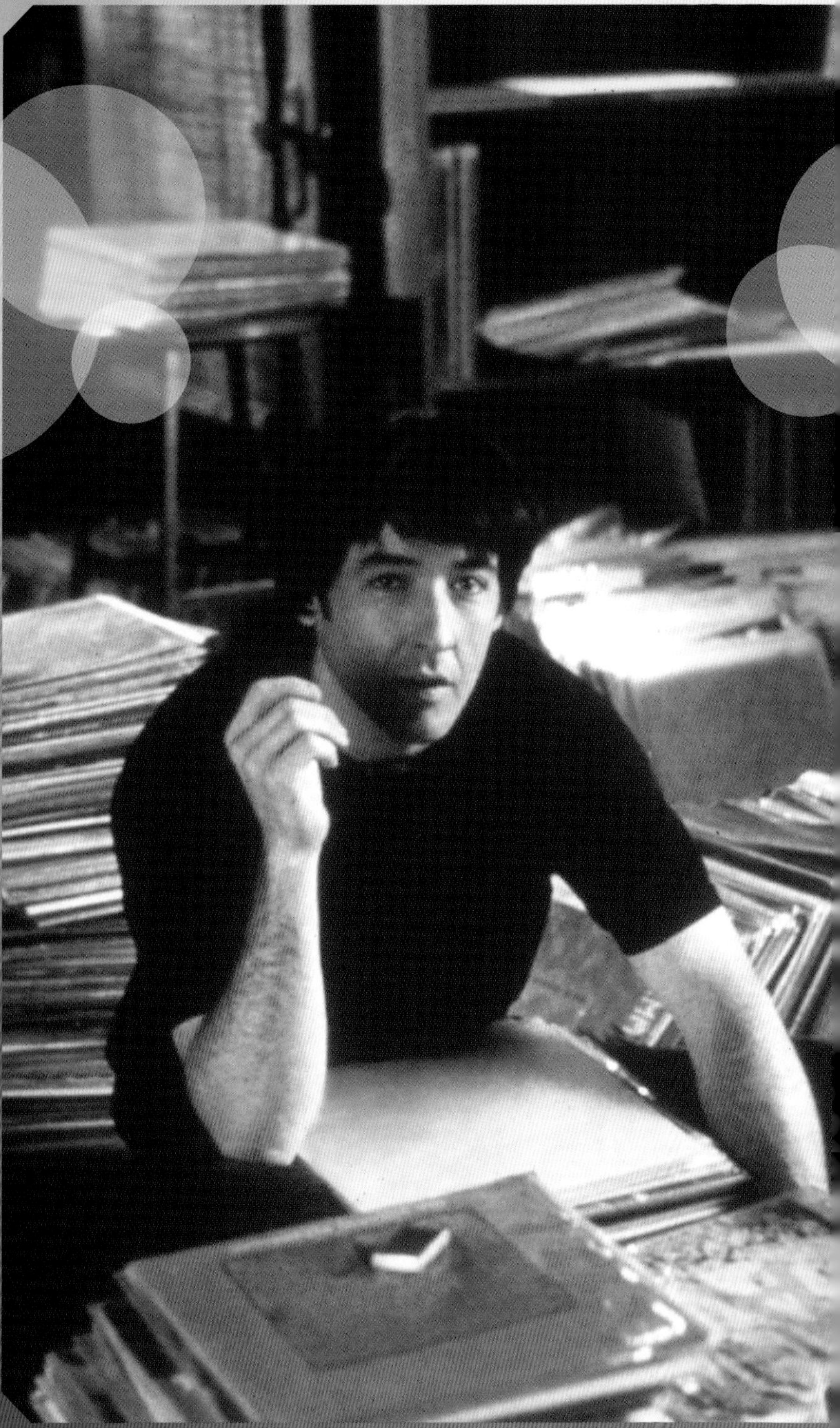

8

THE MAN IN CRISIS

ROM-COMS ARE OFTEN THOUGHT OF AS MOVIES AIMED AT women. So then why are so many rom-coms about men in crisis? Over time the rom-com has proven itself the perfect arena for studying the various insecurities of heterosexual men forced to reckon with their own challenges in the face of potential happiness or love.

If there's an avatar for this subgenre, it's John Cusack. Cusack was not the first person to star in rom-coms about men in crisis, and he certainly wasn't the last, but he somehow is the embodiment of the sad sack dude mired in self-doubt. And if Cusack is the main man in crisis, then *High Fidelity* (2000) is the main man in crisis rom-com.

Based on the book by Nicholas Hornby—another master of male ennui—*High Fidelity*, directed by Stephen Frears, is about a Chicago record store owner, who, after a particularly bad breakup, begins contacting all his exes to see what went wrong. Rob Gordon (Cusack) is bitter and convinced that he was always in the right. He treats the women he's been with like his beloved music collection, sorting them into lists and categories to make sense of his past. The truth? Rob is a huge jerk and, by the end of his project, he's gained at least a modicum of self-awareness and the potential to reunite with the lover who started the whole misbegotten quest.

OPPOSITE: John Cusack as Rob Gordon in *High Fidelity* (2000).

John Cusack and Ione Skye in *Say Anything* (1989).

But let's take a few steps back. Cusack would have never been cast in *High Fidelity* without his breakout role, as Lloyd Dobler, in *Say Anything*. Cameron Crowe's 1989 movie launched Cusack to stardom as the sweetly lovesick high school graduate who becomes infatuated with the gorgeous and brainy Diane Court (Ione Skye). They are severely mismatched. She's off to school in England; all he has planned is kickboxing. You only root for them because of Cusack's effortlessly chill attitude. Lloyd is too young to have Rob Gordon's levels of angst. Still, there's a direct path between these two characters. *Say Anything* goes deeper into Diane's home life—as she becomes disillusioned with her loving but also crooked father—than it does Lloyd's. At the same time, its perspective rests strongly with Lloyd, and we root for him even though there's really no good reason for Diane to be with him. He's nice, yes, but she's a genius. He's someone she'll probably tire of as she sees more of the world.

Rob, meanwhile, is more erudite than Lloyd. He's a man who has defined himself by the culture he consumes and looks down on those who don't have his own encyclopedic knowledge. The commonality between these characters is the essential puppy dog longing that Cusack conveys. They want women they can't or shouldn't have. Lloyd's persistence just happens to come off as charming, while Rob's may make you cringe, even if you potentially relate to him deeply. Men in Crisis are heartsick and wanting. Sometimes, you're totally on their side. Other times, you're not. You're amused by them, but you also realize that their endeavors are a bit ridiculous, the result of ego gone too far. Often these guys have inflated ideas of themselves, which means they try to pursue women who are way out of their reach.

Perhaps the most striking example of this is Billy Wilder's *The Seven Year Itch* from 1955. Based on the play of the same name by George Axelrod, *The Seven Year Itch* is centered on Richard Sherman, played by Tom Ewell. The title refers to a period in a marriage during which a man's gaze starts to stray, and for Richard that happens one summer when he sends his wife and kid off to Maine and he's stuck in the city. The issue is that he has a new neighbor in the upstairs apartment, who just happens to be played by Marilyn Monroe. Her character doesn't even have a name. She's simply "The Girl." Richard goes gaga, as any heterosexual man who sees Marilyn Monroe in the flesh probably would. She's sweet and considers Richard a potential new friend in a strange city. He's driven to distraction by his longing for her.

The ingeniousness of Axelrod and Wilder's script is that it exposes Richard for the fool he is. Yes, Marilyn's presence is fully intended to titillate—after all, this is the film with the sequence where she stands on a subway grate as her white dress billows up against her thighs— but Richard is also depicted as delusional. Much of the movie exists in his head, as he talks to imaginary versions of the women in his life, trying to convince them that he's desirable. Richard walks up to the line of infidelity but never crosses it, and by the end of the movie he's rushing back to his wife and child, realizing what he misses. He does get a kiss from The Girl to send him on his way—the best of both worlds. *The Seven Year Itch* is the account of a man spiraling thanks to his libido before coming to his senses.

The notion of "learning" is often crucial to these fables of misbegotten men. And, as is the case in *The Seven Year Itch*, they often end with the heroes going back to the stable woman in their lives. That is what happens in Blake Edwards's 1979 film *10*, which, like *The Seven Year Itch*, is a movie most associated with an alluring shot of the potential "other woman." Just a smidge less iconic than Marilyn's subway grate peep show is Edwards's image of Bo Derek, hair in cornrows, running on a Mexican beach in a beige bikini. It's the fantasy of a perfect woman who plagues Dudley Moore's songwriter George the same way The Girl lodges herself in the brain of Richard in *The Seven Year Itch*.

In *10*, George has a perfectly lovely relationship with his longtime girlfriend Samantha, played by Edwards's own wife, Julie Andrews. (Why would anyone consider leaving Julie Andrews? Beats me.) Just after celebrating his forty-second birthday, George's car pulls up next to a limo carrying a young woman (Derek) in a wedding gown on a Beverly Hills street. He's utterly taken by this beauty—the picture of a youth he feels slipping away. Like Richard in *The Seven Year Itch*, he becomes obsessed, especially once he learns that that gorgeous woman is the daughter of his dentist. In an act of chaos and desperation, he follows her to the resort in Mexico where she's staying on her honeymoon. He keeps at a distance until he ends up saving her new husband from certain death after the doltish dreamboat falls asleep on a surfboard and drifts out to sea. The woman, whose name turns out to be Jenny, is grateful for George's act of bravery—so grateful that she wants to sleep with him. His fantasy is now staring him in the face. He's surprised to find, however, that she's not some virginal bride. Offered everything he

Tom Ewell lusts after Marilyn Monroe in *The Seven Year Itch* (1955).

wants, George balks, running back into the arms of Samantha. Jenny's youth, the thing he coveted, ultimately terrifies him, and he realizes that he already has everything he ever wanted.

Moore was a king of messy dudes. Just two years later he would star in 1981's *Arthur*, in which he plays a comedically drunk scion of a wealthy family who has never done anything but spend his money on sex workers and booze. His dad plans to cut him off unless he marries an appropriate match, but he falls in love with a woman played by Liza Minnelli, whom he encounters while she shoplifts from Bergdorf Goodman.

There's often a certain morality to these Men in Crisis rom-coms. The romance that the men pursue outside of marriage or whatever is "respectable" leads them back to the place they are supposed to be in society. In 1969's *Cactus Flower*, Walter Matthau is a playboy dentist named Julian Winston who tells his young girlfriend Toni Simmons (Goldie Hawn) that he's married so she won't become emotionally attached to him. The only problem? She's so desperately in love that she attempts suicide. Julian, to mitigate her distress, proposes to her. The only problem is that he now needs a wife to divorce. He enlists his very serious European nurse Stephanie (Ingrid Bergman), a single woman who would be colloquially termed an "old maid," to act as his soon-to-be-ex-spouse. The trouble is, Toni ends up sympathizing with Stephanie and Walter ends up falling in love with the older woman he had never previously considered. By the end of the movie, everyone is paired up with age-appropriate partners.

Even more complicated is a picture like 1973's *A Touch of Class*, which digs into both sides of an adulterous relationship and ends with the central male character heading back to his wife. The film, directed by Melvin Frank, opens with a meet-cute during a park softball game between a suave but obnoxious American (George Segal) and a savvy British fashion designer (Glenda Jackson, who won an Oscar for her work). When he, a married man, proposes an affair to her, a divorced woman, she's open to the idea. She can have fun and stay emotionally distant. Their tryst isn't that easy, however. A getaway to Spain goes awry when one of his friends also happens to be there on vacation with his family, and, on top of that, the lovers' personalities seem to clash immediately. Eventually they reach a sexy détente and start to fall for one another.

As the plot moves forward, these two seem to be headed to something nearing domestic bliss in a rented flat. Except he's still married, and remains so, deciding ultimately to forgo the happiness he has found out of wedlock for something steadier. It's a bittersweet ending. Their coupling was always meant to be brief, but it wasn't meant to have this kind of emotional weight. Unlike in *The Seven Year Itch* or *10*, the traditional marriage our hero goes back to isn't a happy one. He hasn't found solace in his old relationship. Instead, he's simply too afraid of the unknown.

If one of these men does *not* go back to his wife or former girl-friend, it's because she's an unfortunate stereotype of a shrew who doesn't deserve the love a man has to give. In the spirit of *10*, *Forgetting*

Mila Kunis and Jason Segel in *Forgetting Sarah Marshall* (2008).

Sarah Marshall also involves a man fleeing to an exotic locale. In this 2008 film, directed by Nicholas Stoller, from the Apatow school of rom-coms, writer and star Jason Segel plays Peter, a composer for a TV crime procedural who dates the hot star Sarah Marshall (Kristen Bell). She breaks up with him in the film's opening moments and he becomes completely bereft. To try to heal, he heads on a Hawaiian vacation, where it turns out Sarah is also on a trip with her new boyfriend, British pop star Aldous Snow (Russell Brand). Peter sobs in his room while Sarah and her new hottie frolic next door. The chill concierge Rachel (Mila Kunis) is the one who finally helps Peter emerge from his personal pity party, by encouraging him to go cliff jumping and listening to his Dracula musical. She serves as a cool girl counterpart to Sarah's high-maintenance celeb.

It's not that *Forgetting Sarah Marshall* is entirely devoid of nuance. Sarah has every right to break up with Peter, who sits at home doing nothing all day while she works. And Aldous is rather sweet for being a pompous jerk. Rachel isn't entirely a male fantasy either. She too has her own history of bad relationships. At the same time, Peter has a choice between his uptight old flame and the laid-back woman who breaks him out of his shell. The choice to viewers is obvious.

That dichotomy is also evident in another work from director Cameron Crowe, who made Lloyd Dobler in *Say Anything* the ideal broken guy in 1989. Nearly a decade later, Crowe gave us another male romantic comedy hero in the throes of a crisis in the form of Tom Cruise as Jerry Maguire. When 1996's *Jerry Maguire* starts, Cruise's eponymous sports agent is dating a hotshot (Kelly Preston) and at the top of his game. But then he quits his firm, and his world starts to crumble. The one person who stands by his side: an assistant and single mother named Dorothy Boyd, played by Renée Zellweger. If his former lover Avery Bishop was a workaholic demon, Dorothy is almost beatific. She's the only option: the good woman who can save him.

Whether the Man in Crisis is realizing the error of his ways by going back to his longtime partner or he's found a woman who can lift his spirits, this subgenre of rom-com is always essentially about how pitiable a man is and how he needs to be whipped into shape. Love can somehow help him—teach him to be a better person—even if he gets distracted along the way.

PERFECT ROM-COM MOMENT
THE BIRDCAGE (1996)

Mike Nichols's *The Birdcage* is a multilayered movie, but at its heart is a love story between Armand (Robin Williams) and Albert (Nathan Lane) Goldman, a gay couple in a long-term relationship. Their relationship, however, is tested when Armand's son (Dan Futterman) wants to bring home his fiancée (Calista Flockhart), the daughter of a staunch Republican politician. Armand thinks he needs to hide Albert, who is more flamboyant. Feeling unwanted, Albert makes a grand statement, saying he's going to his cemetery, implying he's going to kill himself. Armand meets him on a bench by the water and hands him a piece of paper with a "palimony" agreement, a necessity given that gay marriage was not legal at the time. "I'm fifty years old. There's only one place in the world I call home, and it's because you're there," Armand says. It's love in its truest form.

THE ART OF DECEPTION

GOOD RELATIONSHIPS, WE ARE TOLD, ARE BUILT ON HONESTY. But rom-coms are often built on lies.

My Man Godfrey (1936), one of the earliest screwballs, features a rich man pretending to be poor, who ends up becoming the object of affection of a socialite.

In *Roman Holiday* (1953), Gregory Peck pretends he has no idea who Audrey Hepburn's princess is when he encounters her on the Italian sidewalks. He romances her with the intention of writing a story, even though she just thinks he's a nice stranger. To be fair, she's lying to him too, assuming the identity of a commoner.

Rock Hudson is constantly lying to Doris Day about his identity, pretending to be a gregarious Texan or a nerdy scientist to distract from his real persona, which tends to be of the playboy variety.

Tony Curtis pretends to be a patient of Natalie Wood's young and beautiful psychologist to prove that she's full of it before going gaga for her in *Sex and the Single Girl* (1964).

OPPOSITE: Audrey Hepburn and Gregory Peck tour Rome in *Roman Holiday* (1953).

Kate Hudson and Matthew McConaughey pull a double scam on each other in *How to Lose a Guy in 10 Days* (2003).

These movies all want us to root for these couples to get together by the end. And most of the time they do. It's a bit counterintuitive, which is part of the beauty of rom-com. If a person pulled any of these gambits in real life, you'd probably run away screaming. Call it suspension of disbelief, or maybe more accurately, call it "rom-com logic." In rom-com logic, you can ignore what the lies might say about a person's character if you truly believe the love they feel for their partner. In rom-com logic, you learn to forgive. In rom-com logic, all that matters is reconciliation at the end.

In my opinion, the greatest example of how we learn to accept the worst behavior from people in rom-coms is 1982's *Tootsie*. In *Tootsie*, directed by Sydney Pollack, Dustin Hoffman plays Michael Dorsey, an unsuccessful actor who takes himself way too seriously and can't get hired. When his best friend and onetime fling (Teri Garr) gets an audition for a soap opera, Michael, desperate, decides he's going to audition, in drag, for the role. He wins it and his new persona, Dorothy Michaels, becomes a media sensation. This causes a problem when he falls for Julie Nichols, the beautiful star of the soap, played by Jessica Lange.

Michael is a pest, but Dorothy is a fearless warrior who stands up for women. Dorothy helps Julie fight back against the series' chauvinistic director and she becomes Julie's confidant. Alas, when the ruse is finally up, Julie is furious. She first punches Michael in the groin and then stops talking to him. A little while later, Michael slinks back to her, catching up with her outside the studio. He still loves her and confesses as much. It would appear she's not ready to forgive him, even though she misses Dorothy. Then he hits her with the perfect line: "I was a better man with you as a woman than I ever was with a woman as a man."

It's a good confession, and even if it doesn't fully convince her, she softens a little. They walk away together as she asks if she can borrow

Dustin Hoffman comes clean to Jessica Lange in *Tootsie* (1982).

one of Dorothy's dresses, a yellow Halston number. There's an implication that they will give things a go, and, perhaps surprisingly, you as a viewer find yourself happy with this outcome.

Tootsie has a complicated legacy, to say the least. It operates along a gender binary that doesn't make much sense in the 2020s. It does not give any consideration to transwomen, who wouldn't have been much of a mainstream topic in the 1980s. Hoffman once said that playing Dorothy was a revelation because he was stunned to find he wasn't attractive as a woman. That made him do some self-searching: He concluded that he would never have given Dorothy the time of day if he encountered her in his own life. "There's too many interesting women I have not had the experience to know in this life because I have been brainwashed," he explained.

Knowing all this, it's still possible to be satisfied by the ending. Michael behaved terribly, and while he probably hasn't changed entirely, he is contrite, and I'm willing to believe the experience as

Dorothy did change him a little bit. It's the power of a good performance and an excellent screenplay.

I can't say I feel that way about all the deceptive behavior in romcoms. As much as I love the Day-Hudson movies, I always feel slightly upset by the end of *Lover Come Back* (1961) or *Pillow Talk* (1959). Day never really acquiesces to being with Hudson; she's more forced into complacency by his persistence. On the other hand, when there's an act of mutual deception—as in *Roman Holiday* or *How to Lose a Guy*—you almost feel like the characters deserve each other more. In the former case it's because they are both hiding from a part of themselves; in the latter it's sort of because they are both complicit in the ruse.

Of course, *Tootsie* would have never even been made without its cross-dressing predecessor, Billy Wilder's 1959 classic *Some Like It Hot*, about two jazz musicians (Tony Curtis and Jack Lemmon) who disguise themselves as women to join an all-female musical ensemble to escape mobsters after witnessing a hit. Joe—aka Josephine—(Curtis) is immediately smitten with Sugar, played by Marilyn Monroe, the singer dependent on booze who constantly feels betrayed by men. When they reach their destination in Florida, Joe takes on a third identity—as a millionaire—to woo Sugar, using the yacht owned by Osgood (Joe E. Brown), who has taken a liking to Lemmon's Daphne, otherwise known as Jerry. When Joe thinks his number is up, he takes it upon himself to kiss Sugar, who ends up running away with them and Osgood. Joe tries to implore her to stay away, explaining that he's just the kind of guy who hurt her in the past. She retorts that she's "not very bright," and kisses him. Joe has charmed Sugar as both a man and a woman, but just not as himself, so you believe that she'd be willing to give him a go. At the same time, you also want to shake her and give her some more confidence in herself and her decision.

Meanwhile, when Osgood finally finds out that Daphne is a man, he simply responds, "Nobody's perfect," a line of dialogue that has been etched in history as one of the most famous punch lines.

It's hard to see a future for Osgood and Daphne, specifically because Jerry doesn't seem to be gay. Still, "Nobody's perfect" basically sums up the end of most deception rom-coms. Or most rom-coms in general. The end of the rom-com is about acceptance, even if that means accepting behavior that would otherwise seem like a warning sign.

To love rom-coms is to give yourself over to the idea that lying is part of the game you play to find true love. You would not dare do this in real life—nor should you—but on-screen you have to accept it in all of its recklessness.

Multiple lies are afoot in *Some Like It Hot* (1959).

CHAPTER

10

Sweet, Sweet Fantasy

OFTEN ROM-COMS FEEL LIKE MAGIC. HOW ELSE CAN YOU explain the alchemy of chemistry and coincidence that brings two lovers together and makes it all just *work*? In real life, if Meg Ryan heard Tom Hanks on the radio, stalked him for a while, and then proposed a meetup on the Empire State Building to his young son, he would probably find some way of obtaining a restraining order. And yet somehow it just makes sense in 1993's *Sleepless in Seattle*. You accept the circumstances because Nora Ephron, Hanks, and Ryan draw you in with their charm.

But then there are the rom-coms that rely on *actual* magic. Because of the genre's heightened nature, it is easy to mix supernatural elements into the rom-com stew. Body swaps? Sure! Witches? Of course! Ghosts? Naturally. Time travel? Even better.

Throwing an otherworldly element into the rom-com format often, at least at first, heightens the silliness of the material. Occasionally, however, the element of spirituality deepens the poignancy.

OPPOSITE: Kim Novak, Jimmy Stewart, and a cat named Pyewacket in *Bell, Book and Candle* (1958).

It means there's something that's beyond comprehension for the characters. Love and happiness can come to fruition, but they can also feel tantalizingly out of reach.

While the modern examples of this category can immediately spring to mind—*13 Going on 30* (2004), for instance—writers and directors have been playing around with fantastical elements in love stories for centuries. Does Shakespeare's *A Midsummer Night's Dream* and its multiple film adaptations count? Why, yes!

When *I Married a Witch* was released in 1942 it already came with some fantasy-comedy pedigree. The unfinished novel it was based on, titled *The Passionate Witch*, was written by Thorne Smith, whose *Topper* books had already become a film series starring Cary Grant and Constance Bennett as a pair of perpetually drunken ghosts. In *I Married a Witch*, the bombshell Veronica Lake plays a witch named Jennifer who was burned at the stake by angry Puritans. She returns to the present day as a puff of smoke, aiming to take revenge on Wallace Wooley (Fredric March), the descendant of the man who wronged her. Wallace is at a major moment in his life and career: He's about to get married and is also running for governor. Unbeknownst to him, a meddling witch is about to wreak havoc on his plans. Jennifer plots to making him fall madly in love with her, therefore torpedoing his impending nuptials and political ambitions. He'll ditch his bride-to-be, a scandal will erupt, and he'll lose the election. Except that goes awry when she accidentally takes the love potion she prepares for him and gets all googly-eyed herself. Suddenly, he also finds himself infatuated.

In a *New York Times* review at the time, Bosley Crowther called *I Married a Witch* "spiritualism in a vein of knockabout farce. It is more oh-boy than occult." And while, sure, it's hard to take the actual witchcraft in *I Married a Witch* seriously, it ends up going in the same direction as any number of magical person rom-coms: Will the magic person give up their powers for love? Jennifer confesses her secret

A love potion causes chaos in *I Married a Witch* (1942) with Fredric March and Veronica Lake.

to Wallace, which makes her vulnerable. Her father (Cecil Kellaway) threatens to make her dissolve into thin air again, but it turns out that love is indeed more powerful than any sort of craft—another theme that recurs time and again.

More than a decade later, in 1958, another witch's ill intents are done in by her own love in *Bell, Book and Candle*. Kim Novak plays a seductive Greenwich Village witch who starts toying with the emotions of her neighbor Shep (Jimmy Stewart) upon learning that he is engaged to her college bully. By the end of the film Novak's Gillian is so taken with Shep that she can now cry, meaning she is also a mortal.

Richard Quine's film itself is intoxicating, with hallucinogenic colors and a truly otherworldly, almost dangerous, vibe. The same thing can be said of Novak's performance, which is sensual and menacing.

That's why the ending is ultimately rather disappointing. Can't a woman be a mind-altering witch *and* find the love of her life? In the world of these films, that's rarely the case.

Call it *The Little Mermaid* syndrome. In the Hans Christian Andersen version of the story, the mermaid who longs to be a human doesn't get her man and turns into sea-foam. In the animated Disney version from 1989, she wins the prince but eventually gives up her family and the underwater kingdom she once called home.

This is why the ending of Ron Howard's *Splash*, from 1984, is a refreshing divergence from this trend. There, instead of the mermaid in question, played by Daryl Hannah, abandoning her identity for her love, portrayed by Tom Hanks, she takes him with her into the sea.

During the 1980s, Hanks was the king of the fantasy rom-com with *Splash* and *Big* (1988), the latter of which represents another one of the hallmarks of the subgenre: the body swap and/or transformation. In the Penny Marshall—sister of Garry—movie, Hanks's character begins the film as a child who wishes that he were "big," and suddenly ends up in the body of his thirty-year-old self. He heads to New York and finds himself working for a major toy corporation and ultimately developing a romance with his driven colleague (Elizabeth Perkins), who is charmed by his childlike nature. While this could easily veer into the unsavory, the concept is saved by the brilliance of Hanks's performance. Yes, there's real magic involved in the plot, but there's also the metaphorical magic of Hanks's ability to both fully inhabit the physicality of a twelve-year-old and convey a movie star's charisma, which makes you root for this character to get the girl.

13 Going on 30 has a different approach to the way the magic works. When Jenna (Jennifer Garner) wishes on a dream house during her thirteenth birthday party to be "thirty, flirty, and thriving," she is transported forward in time, immediately inhabiting her own thirty-year-old body in the future. The movie, directed by Gary Winick, derives some of the exact same humor as *Big* does from the idea

Daryl Hannah is a mermaid in *Splash* (1984).

of a thirteen-year-old mind being trapped in a thirty-year-old's body. Jenna is thrilled that she has boobs! She's still freaked out by boys! And there's a charming sort of tension in Jenna realizing who she has become. The thirty-year-old Jenna is nasty—a striver who would screw over her colleagues to get what she wants. She ditched her childhood best friend Matty, now a ruggedly handsome photographer played by Mark Ruffalo, for the popular kids, thus beginning her ascent, or downfall, depending on how you look at it. Garner's performance is a mix of innocent sweetness and genuine fear of what she could become as she seeks to rectify the harm she's caused.

The fantasy elements can often push characters toward realizing that they need to be better people in order to find the love they deserve. Nancy Meyers's hit *What Women Want* (2000) starred Mel Gibson as a playboy who suddenly can hear what women think. At first, he uses his newfound powers for his own benefit, stealing ideas from a coworker (Helen Hunt). Eventually he evolves.

But the king of all Extraordinary Circumstances that Force a Man to Become a Better Person and Find Love fantasy rom-coms happens to be *Groundhog Day*. The 1993 Harold Ramis movie, written by Ramis and Danny Rubin, offers up a genius magical trap to turn grumpy weatherman Phil, played by Bill Murray, into a kind human being. Phil gets stuck in a time loop covering Groundhog Day in Punxsutawney, Pennsylvania, reliving the same aggravating twenty-four hours over and over again. He cycles through emotions regarding his circumstances. He's frustrated, and then he takes advantage of it in nefarious ways, creepily using his foreknowledge of the day's circumstances to hit on his producer Rita (Andie MacDowell). It's not until he finally, truly falls in love with her—and she falls in love with him—that he's released. The time loop is brilliant because it allows Phil to be at both his best and his worst, thus thoroughly convincing the audience of his change by the end of the movie.

Since *Groundhog Day*, the time loop has been deployed on TV and in horror movies, but the best use of it in a rom-com outside of *Groundhog Day* came twenty-seven years later with the release of *Palm Springs* in 2020. *Palm Springs* puts a spin on the time loop by sticking the two love interests in the recurring nightmare together. The initial focus is on Andy Samberg as Nyles, a laid-back dude accompanying his girlfriend to a wedding. They're about to break up—she's obnoxious and cheating on him—but he goes into a magical cave and is stuck repeating the same day. Then the morose sister of the bride, Sarah, played by Cristin Milioti, gets stuck there as well. By the time she arrives in the scenario, he's already figured out all the rules. He's extremely chill, while she's got her own secrets and flaws. She's hooking up with her sibling's husband-to-be and wrestling with that guilt over and over again. Nyles and Sarah fall in love inside their time prison, which becomes a successful metaphor for the ennui of

It takes a long time, but Bill Murray finally time travels enough in *Groundhog Day* (1993) to win over Andie MacDowell.

long-term relationships. She eventually chafes at the metaphysical confinements, whereas he is content to stay locked up.

Fantasy provides a chance to look at the rom-com from a fresh angle. Throw some mysticism into a rom-com format and you can tackle darker concepts while still entertaining the audience. It can be, as in *Palm Springs*'s case, the agony of marriage, or it can be the challenges of grief, as in some other examples.

Adding a dash of magic, if deployed carelessly, can make the stakes of a movie feel weightless. You can feel that in *I Married a Witch*. It's a delightful film, anchored by Lake's sensual glamour, but by the time Jennifer wins the election for Wallace, using her supernatural powers, you start to realize that everything in this universe that is done can be undone and vice versa. But magic can also make a rom-com feel darker or sadder than it might otherwise have. *Bell, Book and Candle* is filled with danger. *Groundhog Day* wrestles with mortality. When you are not bound by the rules of the physical world, anything can happen.

CHAPTER

11

NOT SO HAPPILY EVER AFTER

THE SCREENWRITER MICHAEL H. WEBER PREFERS HOPEFUL endings to happy endings. "The difference being: A hopeful ending is not necessarily that people end up together (although they might), but that they've grown as people," he told me. When Weber was working on the 2009 romantic comedy *(500) Days of Summer* with his writing partner Scott Neustadter, they settled on the hopeful rather than the happy. The central couple—Tom and Summer—do not end up together. Tom has idealized Summer the entire movie, trying to make her into something she's not, even though she very clearly states that she doesn't want a relationship with him. He never ends up convincing her they should be a couple. Instead, they go their separate ways. In the last beat, he ends up meeting another girl, cheekily named Autumn. Is he going to repeat all the errors he made in his tryst with Summer? It's also possible that he's learned something from his experience. That's the sweet spot Weber relishes. "I think, okay, he's not going to make the same mistakes," he says. "He's going to make all new mistakes."

OPPOSITE: Katharine Ross and Dustin Hoffman in *The Graduate* (1967).

Zooey Deschanel and Joseph Gordon-Levitt in *(500) Days of Summer* (2009).

The ending Weber kept looking to for inspiration when making *(500) Days of Summer* was Mike Nichols's *The Graduate* (1967). Benjamin Braddock (Dustin Hoffman) begins an affair with Mrs. Robinson (Anne Bancroft), his parents' friend, and then eventually falls for her daughter Elaine (Katharine Ross), in spite of Mrs. Robinson's warnings to stay away. In the iconic finale, Ben runs to the church where Elaine is getting married and bangs on the window, screaming her name. They run away together and get on a bus—at first happy, then stunned at their decision.

The long take was actually an accident. "I told Dustin and Katharine, 'Look, we've got traffic blocked for twenty blocks, we've got a police escort, we can't do this over and over. Get on the bus and laugh, God damn it,'" Nichols once said. "I remember thinking, What the hell is wrong with me? I've gone nuts. The next day I looked at what we'd shot and went, 'Oh my God, here's the end of the movie: They're terrified.' My unconscious did that. I learned it as it happened."

The Graduate is the not-so-classic girl meets boy—who happens to be having an affair with girl's mom—scenario. And it concludes with the boy and girl running away together. But the sourness in that final shot complicates the triumph of that moment, showing that romantic comedies aren't always quite so tidy.

Indeed, the rom-com has been so often neatly wrapped up in its tropes that the installments complicating the proverbial "ride off into the sunset" ending are seen as outliers. But they are legion and prove that just because romance doesn't always win, that doesn't mean a comedy isn't still romantic in one way or another. These closing moments can be "hopeful," as Weber imagined. Or they can be bittersweet. But they challenge the idea that rom-coms must follow the Shakespearean path of ending a rom-com with a wedding, adding even more depth to the genre.

The last moment of *Roman Holiday* (1953) is like an elegantly delivered punch in the gut. It's gorgeous, but brutal, and thoroughly necessary. Over the course of the film, you've watched Princess Ann (Audrey Hepburn) and journalist Joe Bradley (Gregory Peck) deceive their way into each other's arms. For her, he's the freedom she never had. In his case, her charm melts his hardened exterior.

They must part, however. She goes back to her palatial accommodations, and he returns to the daily drudgery of reporting. Back in their assigned roles, they meet one more time, at a press conference she's hosting. His photographer (Eddie Albert) slips her the negative film strip that documents her wild adventure, and she and Joe clasp hands one final time. She's shocked, but not exactly surprised that he's there. Long after she's exited the stage, director William Wyler's camera lingers on Joe as he leaves the grand hall. They'll never be together. He knows it's not a feasible reality, and yet he holds her memory for just one moment longer before walking off himself.

The provenance of the *Roman Holiday* screenplay is messy. It was attributed on-screen to Ian McClellan Hunter, who won an Academy Award for it, but it was ghostwritten by Dalton Trumbo, who at the time was blacklisted from Hollywood. His screenwriting credit wasn't restored until 2011. Even then, there were apparently other writers who contributed to the film's creation. According to the American Film Institute, the last moments of the movie were rewritten many times, but in what way, it's hard to tell. The Production Code Administration—the body that worked to institute the restrictive Hays Code—used to rate movies according to an "Analysis of Film Content." There were four options for how the reviewer perceived an ending: "Happy," "Unhappy," "Moral," or "Other." *Roman Holiday*'s ending was marked as "Other." That other was: "Self-sacrificing but happy." As with anything in the report, it's a reductive way of looking at a film, but it also feels not quite complete. There is a serenity to the last beats of *Roman Holiday*, to be sure. But it only hits after you've been emotionally walloped. Ann and Joe have both expanded their worldviews for the better, based on their time together. And yet you're left wondering whether they will spend the rest of their lives in a state of regret. Maybe it was just a fling. After all, it only lasted for a single day, really. But there's also a sense that duty can be crushing. The complicated, uneasy

Audrey Hepburn and Gregory Peck know there is no future for them in *Roman Holiday* (1953).

question this iconic romantic comedy asks us is this: How happy is that "self-sacrificing," really?

There are other films in which the sadness of the ending is more implied than spoken, not unlike in *The Graduate*. Billy Wilder's *The Apartment* (1960) falls into that category. Sadness hangs over Billy Wilder's movie about an office cog, C. C. Baxter (Jack Lemmon), and the elevator girl, Fran (Shirley MacLaine), he's mad for. The catch is that Baxter lends out his apartment to the bigwigs at his job so they can have affairs. One of those bigwigs, Mr. Sheldrake (Fred MacMurray), is having an affair with Fran and treating her poorly.

At its heart, *The Apartment* is a rom-com about depression. Fran keeps a broken mirror on her person because it reminds her of how she feels inside. When Baxter looks in it, he recognizes himself in the cracked glass.

Baxter cares for Fran after she attempts suicide, following one of Sheldrake's betrayals. After she's recovered, even though she knows it's a bad situation to be in, she crawls back to Sheldrake. It's not until New Year's Eve that she realizes she can free herself from that cycle. She runs to Baxter's apartment, where she hears a bang, which she mistakes for a gunshot. She bursts in, worrying that he's killed himself. He's just popped some champagne. As they sit on his couch, her coat still on, he confesses his love to her. She hands him a deck of playing cards, saying, "Shut up and deal."

Wilder, who wrote the screenplay with frequent collaborator I. A. L. Diamond, didn't have a finished script when he began filming *The Apartment*. But, as he told director Cameron Crowe in the book of interviews called *Conversations with Wilder*, he and Diamond "always knew our destination." That destination has all the contours of a traditionally "happy" ending—the central couple ends up in the same room together after a dramatic gesture by one of them—but somehow does not fit that narrow description. There's no kiss at the end—a very intentional omission by Wilder. "[Lemmon] could be standing in the window and wave at her, or he opens the door and she kisses him," he once suggested. "We didn't want to have that ending, that kiss ending." With a kiss, *The Apartment* would have been transformed into something it's not: uncomplicatedly sweet.

Fran clearly likes Baxter as a friend, but even as he professes his feelings for her, she's not willing to give him hers in return. Maybe she just doesn't feel that way about him. Or maybe she has realized that she needs to free herself from men in general. She can use a friend at this moment, not a lover. And so, the question then becomes: Does Baxter accept that? And, if so, is he okay with that? That's the beauty of *The Apartment*'s ending. We've left these people in a better place than where they started, but their lives will perhaps always be shaped by disappointment—and we the audience must learn to see the beauty in that as well.

While Cameron Crowe positioned himself as the heir to Wilder's legacy, devoting hours and pages to interviews with the man, one of Crowe's other mentors also took a cue from the likes of *The Apartment* in resolving his unresolvable romances. Like *The Apartment*, 1987's

The triangle of *Broadcast News* (1987).

Broadcast News, written and directed by James L. Brooks, has a heroine whose very personality makes an easy ending all too unlikely.

Brooks's film marries a detailed depiction of the TV news industry with a love triangle comprising Holly Hunter's producer Jane Craig; Albert Brooks's reporter Aaron Altman; and William Hurt's anchor Tom Grunick. Jane's biggest romance is with her work, but her best friend Aaron is desperately attracted to her. Meanwhile, Jane has an ill-advised crush on Tom, a handsome avator of the surface-level journalism she hates. Tom is attracted to her as well, but she's resistant, given how he represents everything she hates. He's just so handsome, though, and Aaron can be so cruel, even in his love.

As the plot nears its close, Jane has essentially chosen Tom, agreeing to go on vacation with him and solidifying their status as a couple. But then she discovers that Tom faked a moment on air—crying during an interview with a date rape survivor. That crosses a line for Jane. She can deal with his other personal failings, but not with him violating journalistic ethics.

Brooks wraps everything up with a coda that takes place some years later. Aaron is married and has a kid. Tom is engaged. Jane mentions a boyfriend. Her real triumph, however, is that she's got a bright, shiny new job in New York. They have all gone their separate ways, probably the better for it.

Brooks did try to do it another way. In an alternate ending that was later released, Tom follows Jane into a car as she leaves the airport. He defends himself: "I can't help it that they like me and I like it that they like me." In their mutual anger, they kiss for a long time. When they separate, she grabs his face. "I could fucking kill you," she says. "You sure could," he says, in an admission of her power. They embrace again.

When they shot that moment, Brooks tried to create something that was purely improvised. He didn't want to tell Hunter that Hurt was getting in her cab. That element of surprise was ruined before the cameras rolled, but the scene still has a looseness of something that wasn't exactly planned. In an interview with MTV News, Brooks called the footage "fascinating." And it is, showing us a less successful attempt at something more conventional in a movie that resists convention.

Sometimes the question at the heart of a romantic comedy is whether or not a protagonist actually deserves to be rewarded at the end of a movie. That's the case with *My Best Friend's Wedding* (1997).

P. J. Hogan's movie always had a problem. Julianne Potter, the character played by Julia Roberts, is mean. To be clear, this is a good thing for the entertainment value. She's a food writer who made a pledge with her best friend Michael (Dermot Mulroney) that they would just up and get married to each other if both remained unhitched by the age of twenty-eight. She's still single when Michael tells her he's marrying a naive college girl named Kimberly Wallace (Cameron Diaz), and Julianne does everything in her power to break up the engagement. She behaves abysmally throughout the course of the movie, practically torturing poor Kimberly and jeopardizing Michael's entire career as a sportswriter in the process. Should she get the man in the end? Honestly, probably not. But should she be punished? Well, I don't know about that either. She *is* Julia Roberts, after all. A grand comeuppance doesn't really seem right either.

Initially, the filmmakers tried an ending where Julianne got a guy. Not *the* guy, but *a* guy. She's seen dancing with a random person—played by John Corbett pre–*Sex and the City* and *My Big Fat Greek Wedding* fame—she meets at the wedding. The implication is that maybe she'll get married too. The filmmakers screened that version for test audiences. The crowd didn't buy it. "The cards basically said, 'Who is this guy she's dancing with at the end? What's she doing with him?'" the screenwriter Ronald Bass told the *Los Angeles Times* upon the film's release. According to Hogan, speaking in a later interview with *Entertainment Weekly*, the viewers, frankly, were still frustrated at Julianne.

Luckily, there was another option. In that original version, Rupert Everett's character George, the Gay Best Friend of Julianne, had hovered in the background of the narrative. Knowing that they needed a new ending, Bass, Hogan, and the producers brought him more to the forefront. Ramping up his role throughout the movie allowed them to center him at the end. Instead of showing Julianne dancing with a person no one had ever seen before, or leaving her completely alone, George shows up, her knight in shining armor. The movie ends with them together. It's not exactly what she wanted, but she's having a pretty good time anyway. And George's presence also softened a difficult character. "That one scene somehow gave the audience permission to forgive Julianne," Hogan told *EW*.

With this maneuver, Everett and the screenplay ultimately made George more than just a side character. And the fact that he likes Julianne, and understands her, allows the viewer to as well. You may not always like this woman's actions, but you can acknowledge her desperation. Sure, she's not getting a man at the end, but she's getting something even better—a person who really loves her. Though *My Best Friend's Wedding* can at times be a very bitter movie, George makes the ending seem not all that ugly. Instead, his and Julianne's dance turns the film into something of a subversive classic.

Rom-coms are often thought of as "comfort food" movies, the kind of things you put on when you're feeling low and need something soothing. And in many ways they are—it's why we love them. But being "comforting" doesn't have to mean being all happy all the time. In many ways, the genre is most interesting when it swerves away from what's expected into something tinged with sadness or wistfulness.

PERFECT ROM-COM MOMENT
BROADCAST NEWS (1987)

What if the guy who doesn't get the girl gets the best moment in the entire movie? That sort of happens in *Broadcast News* when Albert Brooks's Aaron confesses his love for Holly Hunter's Jane. It's clear from the beginning of the film that Jane doesn't see Aaron in that way, but that doesn't stop him from pining for her, even after she's clearly more interested in William Hurt's hunky anchor Tom. Aaron tries to make his case after she comes to see him following the White House Correspondents' Dinner. Tom "personifies everything that you've been fighting against," he says. "And I'm in love with you." She winces—and it tells you everything you need to know about whether this relationship will go forward. "How do you like that? I buried the lede," he adds.

In journalism, "burying the lede" is when you don't start with the most important information. For an audience, it's clear that Aaron is in love, but when it comes time to say it, he puts it below his petty grievances with Tom. All in all, it's a brilliant bit of dialogue and an admission of love that's tinged with pettiness.

12

Rom-Coms and the World

ROM-COMS ARE, OF COURSE, JOYFUL, THE KINDS OF MOVIES you turn to when you want to feel comforted, but at the same time they are not always pure fluff. Not that there's anything wrong with silliness, but in the history of the genre these movies are often more engaged with the greater world around them than their reputation may otherwise suggest.

Yes, the '90s and 2000s rom-com often existed out of time, in a fantasy version of whatever city it was set in. The New York of, say, *Maid in Manhattan*, which was released in 2002, didn't really feel like the post-9/11 New York most residents experienced, even though it was supposed to be about a romance between a Republican politician and a Latina hotel maid.

Still, if you look at a broader picture of rom-coms, you'll find that these movies are frequently responding to the historical period in which they are set. There are rom-coms that deal with politics. There

OPPOSITE: Jean Arthur, John Lund, and Marlene Dietrich posing for *A Foreign Affair* (1948).

are rom-coms that deal with war and financial collapse. And while they often do so with a dash of fantasy, they also emerge from the real, sometimes troubling climates surrounding them.

The 1936 version of *My Man Godfrey*, based on the novel by Eric Hatch, begins in a shantytown. A group of obnoxious rich people on a scavenger hunt, in party clothes, are gallivanting around this wasteland of poverty looking for a "forgotten man." Cornelia Bullock (Gail Patrick), who is particularly snooty, encounters Godfrey (William Powell), one such person, and offers him $5 if he'll return with her to the swanky venue where the hunt is headquartered and help her win. Having some dignity left, he says no and pushes her. This absolutely tickles her sister Irene (Carole Lombard), who is used to getting trampled by Cornelia. Finally, someone said no to her. Sensing Irene's kindness—and wanting to rib Cornelia even further—Godfrey offers to accompany Irene and help her win the prize. At the end of the night, much to Cornelia's chagrin, Irene offers Godfrey a job.

While the idea of making a sport out of poor people's fates sounds improbably cruel to our modern ears, this plot was based on a real tradition started in 1933 by the gossip columnist Elsa Maxwell at the Waldorf-Astoria. The catch in the film is that Godfrey is not actually a bum. Instead, he's a Harvard graduate who, after a heartbreak, decided to go live among the country's poor, despite his wealth. Over the course of the screwball affair, Irene falls hopelessly in love with Godfrey, who tries to shun her affections to protect his job and his identity. By the end, however, Godfrey decides to give up the ruse and use his riches to transform the homeless encampment by the East River into a rollicking nightclub, employing the "forgotten men" in the meantime. Irene is, of course, even more enchanted by him and brings a priest to his office so they can marry on the spot.

In some ways, *My Man Godfrey* is more satirical than it is romantic. Lombard is a fizzy joy, but the sparks never truly fly between Irene

The scavenger hunt prize in *My Man Godfrey* (1936).

and Godfrey, who is unaffected by her attempts at wooing. The film, directed by Gregory La Cava, is about the irrepressible kookiness of the Bullocks in a time of a national crisis. Upon release, it was called "exuberantly funny" in the *New York Times* by critic Frank S. Nugent. But when *My Man Godfrey* was remade in 1957 with June Allyson and David Niven, the then-critic for the *Times*, Bosley Crowther, questioned whether it was even still relevant. "Back in the Nineteen Thirties, when 'My Man Godfrey' was first made, we were still getting over the Depression and very few people had much wealth. Therefore, it was easy to get people to laugh at a satire of the rich, to believe that the wealthy could be quite whacked and to appreciate a poor man's dignity," he wrote. He continued: "But today lots of people are wealthy and the rest are not averse to that idea. It's hard to believe that

Ninotchka, played by Greta Garbo, tries to square her Communist ideals with eating in a Parisian restaurant.

anybody—least of all a handsome, charming gentleman—should be compelled by circumstances to be a bum." Crowther's comments exude a midcentury optimism that seems rather silly decades later, when the wealth gap in America once again looks like a vast chasm. Still, it is poignant commentary on the ways in which a rom-com must meet its own political moment.

It's hard to imagine that twenty-first-century filmmakers could get away with the flippancy with which *My Man Godfrey* regards

Depression-era poverty, and yet the movie now feels less like the fluff it was regarded as in its day and more like something almost radical.

Three years after the original *Godfrey* premiered, World War II broke out in Europe, and the romantic comedy once again wrestled with its era. *Ninotchka*, which was released in 1939, both distances itself from the war that was raging abroad and centers itself in political conversation. After the credits run at the outset of Ernst Lubitsch's film, a title card reads: "This picture takes place in Paris in those wonderful days when a siren was a brunette and not an alarm . . . and if a Frenchman turned out the light it was not on account of an air raid!" It's a positively jolly way to address the fact that there's a horrific conflict going on. And yet despite that cheeriness, the film itself plunges the audience into a comedy about Communism.

The film begins with three Soviet emissaries arriving in Paris to sell lavish jewels belonging to a former Russian aristocrat for the benefit of their cause. These men are immediately lured by the comforts of Parisian luxury. The grand duchess, Swana (Ina Claire), to whom the gems once belonged, gets word of their presence. She dispatches her lover, Leon (Melvyn Douglas), also a former aristocrat, to retrieve her confiscated belongings. And then Ninotchka arrives. Ninotchka, portrayed by Greta Garbo in what was hailed as a groundbreaking comedic role, is the human embodiment of the Soviet idea. She chides her comrades for their behavior with deadpan seriousness. Despite their differences, Leon is smitten with Ninotchka and attempts to woo her, though he finds himself battling up against her strident, austere nature. Ninotchka finds herself giving in—not wholly, but just a little, to his charms. Ninotchka is a classic high-maintenance woman, only her specific personal customs are born out of life under Communism and a loyalty to the cause.

Lubitsch was German-born to a Russian father and had strong negative feelings about the Communist society in Russia, according to his biographer Scott Eyman. A honeymoon trip to the country with his wife, Vivian Gaye, cemented his disdain. Eyman writes about Lubitsch's reaction when the wife of a former colleague expounded on Soviet virtues: "So this was what had replaced the dirt and squalor of czarist Russia from which his father had escaped! He could understand why the lower and working classes preferred life under communism—it held the promise of improvement. But for an artist?" *Ninotchka* is an expression of that perspective, just in rom-com packaging.

Though Ninotchka's communist tendencies bear the brunt of the jokes in the film—which was co-written by Billy Wilder—it spares some of its punch lines for capitalist greed as well. In the iconic restaurant scene in which Leon attempts with all his might to get Ninotchka to laugh, he is seen as much as a fool, if not more so, than she is. The establishment they walk into is the kind of place where neither of them belongs, exactly. For Ninotchka, any spot where people get joy from eating and drinking is foreign. Meanwhile, Leon usually frequents fancier venues. His attempts at humor fail—that is, until he falls on the floor and the entire room, Ninotchka included, bursts out laughing.

Three years later, Lubitsch's work would get even more explicitly responsive to the times with 1942's *To Be or Not to Be*. This spoof of Nazi incompetence is set among a group of actors in Warsaw, who go undercover to foil Hitler's emissaries. It's also a rom-com about a married pair of performers (Carole Lombard and Jack Benny) and the jealousy he feels when she starts inviting a handsome young pilot backstage during his soliloquy. *To Be or Not to Be* is now largely regarded as a classic, landing thirteenth on the BBC's list of the greatest comedies of all time, along with other rom-coms like 1959's *Some Like It Hot* (number one) and 1977's *Annie Hall* (number three).

But at the time, it was not well received. Actor Robert Stack told Eyman: "The press did a terrible number on Lubitsch and the arrogance he supposedly had in making fun of the Polish situation. But he was a Jew from the Old Country himself!" Bosley Crowther of the

Jean Arthur as Connie with Charles Coburn as her houseguest Dingle in *The More the Merrier* (1943).

New York Times called it a "callous comedy," angered, seemingly, that Lubitsch tried to present the grim realities of living in occupied Poland, along with his typical zippy romantic storylines.

Crowther had no such issues with *The More the Merrier*, which was released the following year, which he called "as warm and refreshing a ray of sunshine as we've had in a very late Spring." Perhaps the grim conditions on the home front were more appropriate for light humor, in Crowther's opinion. Directed by George Stevens, who would eventually film some of the most resonant footage from D-Day as well as the Dachau and Duben concentration camps, *The More the Merrier* takes wartime hardship and the D.C. housing crisis and turns it into a romantic comedy about a woman, Connie (Jean Arthur), who rents out a room in her apartment to an elderly gentleman, Benjamin Dingle (Charles Coburn), who in turn rents out half of his share to a suave, no-nonsense sergeant, Joe Carter (Joel McCrea). Already frustrated with the fact that her tenant is Mr. Dingle—she wanted a woman, and Dingle does not follow her precise instructions for cohabitation—Connie is even more outraged when she learns that she's shacking up with a second man. But Dingle sees sparks where Connie initially doesn't and plays matchmaker for his two roommates, even though Connie happens to be engaged to a stuffy bigwig named Charles Pendergast (Richard Gaines).

The More the Merrier is a World War II rom-com that stays far away from the horrors of war. Instead, it finds its characters in the patriotic men and newly employable women who flocked to the nation's capital with a do-gooder spirit. Even if places to live and eligible bachelors were scarce, these industrious folks were there to help America no matter what the cost. The logline for the movie could have come from a 1942 article in *Good Housekeeping*, reprinted later by the *Washington Post*: "There's a new army on the Potomac—the bright-eyed, fresh-faced young Americans who have poured into Washington from remote farms, sleepy little towns, and the confusion of cities, to work for the government in a time of national emergency. Every morning they flow, like bright rivers, into the maws of the great buildings."

But Jean Arthur's Connie Milligan is not the kind of wide-eyed naïf that description would suggest. Since she has lodging to begin with, it is implied that she was there long before the crowds descended—a government lifer who isn't desperately searching for a man the way some of her peers are. In fact, she already has a fiancé and is dragging her feet when it comes to the actual wedding. That relationship with a classic Baxter just happens to get tested by the sexy soldier Joe Carter. Even though *The More the Merrier* deftly adheres to the production codes of the time, sexuality hovers over it. Joe and Connie are just a room away from each other, their hormones drawing them closer together. At the same time, the jolly presence of Coburn means the whole film has a goofy sweetness. In fact, it was Coburn as Dingle who was the breakout star: In a 1945 profile of Coburn in *Movieland*, author Dorothy Deere wrote: "The 'Dingle' is a kind of inner laughter which wraps itself around the affections of women both young and old and causes them to characterize Mr. Coburn as 'cute.'"

After the release of *The More the Merrier*, Stevens went overseas as part of a film unit to capture the fighting and atrocities, bringing back images that were worlds away from the cheery optimism of the feature just described. Three years after the end of the conflict, Billy Wilder embedded some of the actual ruins of World War II into his romantic comedy *A Foreign Affair*. The 1948 film, also starring Jean Arthur, opens with footage of the rubble of Berlin. "It was absolute ashes, Berlin," said Wilder in a later interview.

In *A Foreign Affair*, Arthur plays Republican congresswoman Phoebe Frost, who comes to Berlin to check up on the state of US troops. She's a stickler for American values and is shocked to find what she considers a moral cesspool—US soldiers shacking up with locals, selling goods on the black market, and frequenting underground clubs. When she gets wind that one service member is involved with Nazi ally Erika Von Schlütow, played in appropriately sultry fashion by Marlene Dietrich, she recruits Captain John Pringle (John Lund), whom she pegs as a good boy from Iowa, to help her suss out the rapscallion. The only problem: Pringle is the one sleeping with Von Schlütow, so he decides to seduce Phoebe to knock her off the scent. *A Foreign Affair* is as much a love story between Pringle, who ends up falling for his mark, and Frost as it is a portrait of a city reeling in the

John Lund as Captain Pringle in the rubble of Berlin in *A Foreign Affair* (1948).

wake of its destruction and the lingering effects of Nazism. Though it ends with Pringle and Phoebe together, it's ultimately a rather cynical film, with a bite to it.

The representative for the Hays Code administration was positively aghast at an early draft of that script co-written by Wilder. "We believe this material presents a very serious problem of industry policy with regard to the characterization of the members of the Congressional Committee and of the members of the American Army of Occupation," one Stephen S. Jackson wrote. On top of the potential offense to government bodies, Jackson was also fearful about the "overemphasis on illicit sex," which, yes, is crucial to the plot. It's not that those worries were allayed by the time of release. Crowther, in a positive *New York Times* review wrote: "Congress may not like this picture, which came to the Paramount yesterday. And even the Department of the Army may find it a shade embarrassing." It remains, however, one of the most boldly edgy romantic comedies of all time, steamy and angry, highlighting not just the war criminals who haunted postwar Berlin but also the ineffectualities of American occupation.

As the United States entered times of postwar prosperity, the romantic comedy frequently reflected that too. The rom-coms of the decades that followed turned to ever-present gender politics, though they often eschewed reflecting the world beyond their tiny dramas. Naturally, there are exceptions to that rule, though. One might consider Hal Ashby's *Shampoo* (1975), about a sultry Hollywood hairdresser played by Warren Beatty. *Shampoo* takes place against the backdrop of Richard Nixon's election and is a sly commentary on the sexual mores of the Beverly Hills biddies Beatty is wooing.

You can also look to more diverse rom-coms for examples of films that address the realities of an era. In 1974, Diahann Carroll starred opposite James Earl Jones in *Claudine*, which is specifically about the economic struggles of a Black woman in Harlem in the 1970s. Claudine, played by Carroll, is a mother of six who is on welfare, which is not nearly enough to survive on, so she works as a maid for a white family in Riverdale, a middle-class neighborhood in the Bronx. There she is wooed by a charming garbage collector, Rupert (Jones). Rupert, who goes by Roop, just wants to treat Claudine right, but bringing a man into the picture would create a whole new set of problems for Claudine, who has to continually prove that she is single to qualify to get money from a government that doesn't really care about her plight.

Claudine is a courtship entirely concerned with the struggles of its main characters' existence, down to the angst of Claudine's children, including one who is eager to get into radical politics and another who is engaged in a relationship that Claudine worries would result in another mouth to feed. And yet, despite all that, the audience is still thoroughly engrossed in Claudine and Roop's own affair.

Claudine is a rarity, and it seemed the more popular the rom-com became later in the twentieth century, the less interested it became in dealing with the actual issues of the day. In the '90s and 2000s heyday of the rom-com, the fantasy took hold even when the film wrestled with politics. Even Ivan Reitman's 1993 White House–set *Dave*, about a look-alike who inadvertently becomes president, has the starry-eyed attitudes of the first half of that decade. More recently, some rom-coms have actively engaged with hot-button issues, among them 2014's *Obvious Child*, in which the heroine, played by Jenny Slate, has a one-night stand that results in an unwanted pregnancy. She decides to terminate it but ends up still being pursued by the man involved, resulting in an emotionally complicated situation.

The truth is: Idle viewers don't give this genre enough credit for the commentary it can make within confines that are otherwise viewed as snuggly. Whether it's a movie like *My Man Godfrey*, mocking the people who make fun of the Depression, or *Obvious Child*, weaving a hot-button issue into an otherwise adorable coupling, there's no reason to discount the rom-com by saying it exists entirely in la-la land. Sure, some of them do, but there are quite a few that want to use love to engage in timely conversations.

PERFECT ROM-COM MOMENT
CLAUDINE (1974)

Yes, it's nice when a date will wine and dine you, but what if the most romantic thing they could do is to just draw you a bath and let you relax? That's what happens in *Claudine*. Garbage man Roop (James Earl Jones) wants to take out domestic worker Claudine (Diahann Carroll), but her house is filled with her children and there's no hot water. So he invites her over for a bath at his place before they head to dinner. He has no ulterior motives in that moment. He just wants her to relax. And relax she does. She falls asleep in the bubble bath and they miss their chance to go out to eat. But Roop doesn't care. All he wants is her happiness. Is your heart melting now?

In *Claudine* (1974), James Earl Jones orchestrates a perfect low-key date for Diahann Carroll.

TEENAGE DREAMS

ONE OF AMERICAN SCREENWRITER KELLY FREMON CRAIG'S earliest rom-com memories is Molly Ringwald, her face lit by birthday candles, sitting on a table and leaning in for a kiss with Jake Ryan. (The actor's name is Michael Schoeffling, but he is, in perpetuity, the hunky Jake Ryan.) The scene is at the end of *Sixteen Candles* (1984), the first of John Hughes's high school rom-coms, and the one that gave awkward girls everywhere the hope that they could end up kissing the hottest senior in school.

Thirty-two years later, Craig made her own high school movie, *The Edge of Seventeen* (2016), in which a teen even more awkward than Molly Ringwald's Sam Baker—Hailee Steinfeld's Nadine Franklin—spirals after finding out her best friend is dating her popular twin brother, whom she hates. You can see Hughes's DNA all over *The Edge of Seventeen*, which takes his template and propels it into an era when the heroine gets to be just a bit messier.

Craig, for her part, never really understood the appeal of Jake. Jake is traditionally handsome, with high cheekbones and higher hair. He's a suave, popular guy with a beautiful blonde girlfriend. Why does Sam like him? Mainly because he's hot.

OPPOSITE: Molly Ringwald and Michael Schoeffling in *Sixteen Candles* (1984).

Hughes set the template for the high school rom-com in 1984 and, in the decade that followed, the subgenre would explode. These movies operate at the intersection between the coming-of-age film and the classic romantic comedy. "I do think on some level the coming-of-age experience is about feeling seen," Craig said in an interview. "And maybe on some level the rom-com is operating in a similar way in that you find somebody who sees you and loves you for who you are."

Craig is right that high school and the rom-com make a good match. Rom-coms already happen on heightened planes of existence, where emotions are bigger than they are in real life. In high school everything already *feels* more dramatic, which makes it a perfect setting for a romantic comedy to unfold. In the high school rom-com, you are almost certain that these relationships aren't going to last forever. In fact, they may not even last five minutes after the credits roll. But you're willing to invest in them because you know how potent early love is.

The high school movie, and, with it, the high school rom-com, didn't start in the '80s with John Hughes. The American teenager started to take hold of popular culture in the late 1950s. In a 1959 story in the *Los Angeles Mirror*, an article declared: "If you think there are more motion pictures aimed at youngsters, you're right. Appeal to the crew cut set is foremost in most producers' minds these days. That's because movie houses' best customers are under 21 years old." The following years were littered with "beach party" flicks, featuring Sandra Dee and Annette Funicello in bikinis on the sand, as they are wooed by men in tiny shorts.

But the '80s were when the teen rom-com really started to develop, and that was mostly thanks to Hughes, who gave his on-screen kids the sadness and the passion that they had previously lacked in the bubbly '60s.

A year before *Sixteen Candles* came out, Martha Coolidge released *Valley Girl* (1983), a paean to 1980s Los Angeles culture. It's a classic "girl falls for boy from the wrong side of the tracks" story, in which a privileged girl from the San Fernando Valley (Deborah Foreman) is pursued by a rough-around-the-edges guy (Nicolas Cage). Coolidge's movie itself is sort of like its hero. It has a rocking soundtrack and gorgeously filmed sequences of driving around the city that inspired its title, but it's a little jagged, with tepid chemistry between its two leads.

Hughes's magic trick was making his teens feel like real teens. That was in part thanks to the casting of Ringwald and Anthony Michael Hall, who at the time of release were really sixteen. Their vulnerability shines through. In *Sixteen Candles*, Ringwald's Sam Baker doesn't have great options. But, regardless of how you feel about the dudes, you want Sam to get the guy because Ringwald plays her with such lived-in longing.

Jon Cryer and Molly Ringwald in *Pretty in Pink* (1986).

Ringwald herself was impossibly adorable, the kind of person with the poise and looks that would make you assume she is more like her character in *The Breakfast Club* (1985), a popular girl whom everyone loves. But Sam Baker is ignored, and you see the pain of being overlooked in Ringwald's frustrated portrayal. The boy she likes is out of her league and even her parents have forgotten her birthday. It's the ultimate teen indignity.

Sixteen Candles has well-documented problems. The Asian character of Long Duk Dong is a racist stereotype, and the film includes a miserable date rape joke. But we keep returning to it because of Ringwald's relatable longing that anyone who has been a lovesick teen can understand.

Ringwald carried that quality into her collaboration with Hughes two years later in *Pretty in Pink* (1986), directed from Hughes's script by Howard Deutch, which cast her as another teen outcast, but this one with a greater sense of self-possession. Andie Walsh knows exactly who she is. She lives on the literal wrong side of the tracks with her out-of-work father, and while she doesn't have a lot of money she has a distinct sense of style, evident in the floral outfits she crafts herself. This makes her a target of the rich kids in school, with their perfect hairdos and polo shirts. It doesn't stop her from falling head over heels in love with one of those "richies"—Blane, played by Andrew McCarthy. He adores her too, as does Duckie (Jon Cryer), with whom she shares a lack of means and a love of hats.

Duckie follows in the footsteps of movie dorks before him but becomes his own archetype because he's just *so* desperate. He's not quite a Baxter because Andie never really entertains the idea of dating him, and he barely counts as a Best Friend because Andie doesn't even seem to like him very much. There are fans who argue that Andie should have ended up with Duckie, even though his behavior is downright stalker-esque, but that mostly has to do with the fact that he's more interesting than Blane and can do a pretty good lip sync.

Even though the Hughes movies shined light on the weirdos and outsiders of the high school scene, they are all ultimately deeply traditional in tone. Sam gets the guy. Andie ends up at prom, even though she is skeptical about whether she wants to go. If you are one of those weirdos or outsiders, you might possibly see through the conservatism inherent in their happy endings, or you might just love it anyway. I was in the latter camp. I was a school-obsessed dork who didn't kiss a boy until I got to college, but still had fantasies of showing up at prom in an ugly, handmade dress I thought was beautiful, with the perfect boy running after me.

That's also the fantasy of the high school rom-com. These people may kiss at the end of the movie, but any reasonable adult knows that they will likely break up by the time they get to college. That tension exists in *Say Anything* (1989). When Diane and Lloyd end up on a plane together—him tagging along with her—there's a *Graduate*-like dread in the turbulence that hits the flight. Then the ride suddenly becomes smooth, offering a bit of relief for the audience and the characters. It's hard to ignore the bumpy road these two will probably face.

At the same time, ridiculousness is sort of the point. In high school you can have big dreams and it doesn't matter if they are totally unrealistic.

Hughes was a force in his own right, but he was also setting the stage for the teen rom-coms of the 1990s and early 2000s. It's tough to argue that Hughes's work was quaint in any way—his characters drank alcohol and had sex—but they had a gentler touch than many of their '90s counterparts. Many of the '90s favorites of the genre maintained some of Hughes's traditional values—these movies often remained convinced that a girl needs to take off her glasses and put on some makeup to be beautiful—but they also could feel less personal, the stars more polished without that truly youthful charm of Ringwald.

The filmmakers of the era also figured out a key fact about high school movies. The big emotions can be easily mapped on to classic texts. These cheeky reinterpretations of Jane Austen and Shakespeare understand that the best rom-coms have a timeless quality, so why not just borrow from some of the most timeless works of literature?

The queen of all these movies is Amy Heckerling's *Clueless* (1995), which moves the general plot of Jane Austen's *Emma* to Beverly Hills. Instead of Emma Woodhouse, we have Cher Horowitz. Both are equally self-centered young women who think they can fix everything with their charm.

Clueless is brilliant, with Heckerling understanding that Austen's wry observations about social class are just as relevant to a bourgeois

Alicia Silverstone as Cher and Paul Rudd as her ex-stepbrother, Josh, in *Clueless* (1995)—a couple bizarrely meant to be.

high school experience in the rich enclaves of Los Angeles as they are to nineteenth-century England. And instead of mimicking the style of Austen's speech, Heckerling invented her own way of speaking—a spin on the Valley Girl dialect, even if Cher and her posse would rather die than go to the Valley.

Cher, like Emma before her, thinks she can fix other people's lives instead of her own, so she ignores her own romantic endeavors until she cannot deny them any longer. She pursues a new kid in town, named Christian, who happens to be gay, and then ultimately realizes that she's "butt-crazy" in love with her ex-stepbrother, Josh, the college boy played by Paul Rudd. Because she's not interested in the pursuit so much, as her love suddenly dawns on her, their easy rapport is more charming than many contrived attempts at chemistry. The ingeniousness of *Clueless* is that it takes the Regency-era gender and class politics of Austen's world and transposes them onto the Los Angeles elite of the 1990s. They may not have estates, but they have mansions and BMWs and they wear the haute-couture brand Alaïa.

A classic author even riper for translation is Shakespeare, the great-grandfather of the rom-com plot. The tropes that he relied on in the sixteenth and seventeenth centuries are easily transferrable to any scenario. Cross-dressing? See *As You Like It* or *Twelfth Night*. Romance as a contest? He was there—Shakespeare predated, to understate things greatly, *She's All That*, the 1999 teen rom-com in which Rachael Leigh Cook angrily asks, "Am I a bet?"

So in the 1990s and 2000s, looking for plots, rom-com writers transposed Shakespeare's words onto high school kids. Thematically, it's evocative. The students who are being forced to read these texts for their English classes are now acting out the very scenarios that were relevant generations ago.

The Taming of the Shrew might have aged the most poorly of Shakespeare's comedies. It's a story about an independent woman being (literally in the original text) beaten into falling in love with a man who takes on the task of subduing her for monetary reasons. And yet the plot was revisited twice between 1999 and 2003. In 2003, *Deliver Us from Eva* cast Gabrielle Union as the strict leader of a group of three sisters, all of whom have boyfriends who are frustrated by Eva's ways. They convince a local playboy (LL Cool J) to seduce her (for a fee) to get her off their hands. Before that, in 1999, *The Taming of the Shrew* went to high school in *10 Things I Hate About You*, written by Karen McCullah and Kirsten Smith, and directed by Gil Junger.

Julia Stiles plays Kat Stratford—the names are nods to Shakespearean locations—the terrifying feminist of her high school. Her younger sister Bianca (Larissa Oleynik) is a perky popular girl desired by boys, but their father has determined that Bianca can only date if Kat does. Enamored of Bianca, nerd Cameron (Joseph Gordon-Levitt) pays new-to-town rebel Patrick Verona (Heath Ledger) to woo Kat. Feelings develop all around.

10 Things I Hate About You avoids the pesky paternalistic pitfalls of Shakespeare's original work by never making Kat give up her strident beliefs, even as she is ultimately charmed by Patrick. (And it's hard not to be, given how Ledger, an Australian newcomer at the time, was at the peak of his heartthrob powers.) But Kat's a recognizable type, a high school girl who has taken solace in *The Bell Jar* and her own angst. Falling in love with Patrick never seems like a betrayal of her ideals. He's another oddball outcast after all.

Even more Shakespeare-inspired teen rom-coms followed. In 2001, *Get Over It* used *A Midsummer Night's Dream* as a backdrop for goofy love triangles, focusing on a lovesick boy (Ben Foster) who joins the cast to get his girlfriend back, only to fall for the singer-songwriter played by Kirsten Dunst. Then 2006 brought *She's the Man*, a *Twelfth Night* rip-off, in which former child star Amanda Bynes dresses up as a boy to join a soccer team.

Heath Ledger and Julia Stiles bond in the Shakespearean riff *10 Things I Hate About You* (1999).

Of course, there are also straightforward adaptations of both Austen and Shakespeare, not set in high school, that can fully qualify as rom-coms. In addition to *Clueless* there have been multiple *Emmas*, including one in 1996 starring Gwyneth Paltrow, just a year after *Clueless*'s release, and another with Anya Taylor-Joy decades later in 2020. The 2005 adaptation of *Pride and Prejudice*, starring Keira Knightley, is beloved. As for the Bard, Kenneth Branagh made a faithful take on *Much Ado About Nothing* in 1993. In 2013, there was a stripped-down *Much Ado*, directed by Joss Whedon, that nevertheless used Shakespeare's language.

But while these faithful takes on the material are well done, I sometimes prefer the versions set on campuses. There's something thrilling about throwing an old story into a new context.

The young-adult trends of the late 2000s and 2010s moved away from rom-coms. The movies that aimed to capture teen audiences were less interested in funny scenarios and more interested in vampires (*Twilight*) and battles to the death (*The Hunger Games*). But in 2018 something shifted with the release of a rom-com based on a YA novel called *To All the Boys I've Loved Before*.

That year felt like something of a turning point in the rom-com world. On the big screen *Crazy Rich Asians* became the first rom-com to break through at the box office in years, grossing over $239 million worldwide. But, on the small screen, *To All the Boys*, which streamed on Netflix, became a competing phenomenon.

Based on a novel by Jenny Han, *To All the Boys* tells the story of Lara Jean Covey (Lana Condor), a girl who loves romance but is deeply shy. Whenever she has a crush, she writes the object of her affection a detailed, gushy letter and stores it away in a box in her room. Alas, things go sideways for Lara Jean when her little sister decides to mail those letters. One lands in the hands of hunky lacrosse player Peter Kavinsky (Noah Centineo), who, rather than rejecting her, befriends Lara Jean and eventually asks her to start fake-dating to make his ex-girlfriend mad. Lara Jean's crush is still potent and the feeling is, in the long run, reciprocated.

To All the Boys was not just a hit by the metric of viewership—it felt like a genuine pop culture moment. Lara Jean's girly, floral aesthetic was made to be picked up by Instagram, and Noah Centineo emerged as an immediate heartthrob.

But the movie also felt revelatory because of its half-Asian lead heroine. The high school rom-coms before were mostly white, and when Asian characters appeared they were either relegated to the background or cast as stereotypes, as in *Sixteen Candles*. As Han said in an interview: "We've seen a certain type of rom-com many times, and I have never seen an Asian American girl as the lead of a rom-com. So I think being able to experience the first blush of first love through her eyes, it felt really new and sparkly."

To All the Boys generated two sequels, neither of which could quite capture the buzz of the first movie. Still, even just making it to those sequels felt like both a throwback and a shift change. If Lara Jean Covey could win hearts, so could many other leads who don't look like the '80s or '90s teen rom-com stars.

PERFECT ROM-COM MOMENT
CLUELESS (1995)

Sometimes the "aha" moment is almost as gratifying as the first kiss. Cher Horowitz (Alicia Silverstone) knows this. The most euphoric moment in *Clueless* comes when Cher realizes she is "majorly, totally, butt-crazy in love with Josh," her adorable ex-stepbrother, played by Paul Rudd. She's on a Beverly Hills shopping spree—her way of coping after a drag-out argument with her friend Tai (Brittany Murphy), wherein Tai told her she has a crush on Josh. Prowling those Southern California blocks in a miniskirt, suddenly it dawns on Cher. She is the one who loves Josh. The music swells, and the fountain behind her starts to spurt to the sky, the lights inside it changing colors. Then we get a montage of all the flirtatious moments Cher and Josh have shared up until this point, and we realize it too. We are butt-crazy in love with them.

CHAPTER 14

LGBTQ+ LOVE

"BECAUSE I JUST WENT GAY ALL OF A SUDDEN," CARY GRANT says in *Bringing Up Baby* (1938), wearing a frilly nightgown. The line of dialogue was famously improvised by Grant, playing a mild-mannered paleontologist driven to near insanity by Katharine Hepburn's heiress Susan, who has made off with his clothing, thus forcing him to wear the fur-accented sleepwear. Asked why he is dressed in the feminine attire by Susan's Aunt Elizabeth (May Robson), who is befuddled by his presence in her home, he blurts out that exclamation.

"I just went gay all of a sudden" may have been the first time *gay* was used to mean homosexual in film history, but the rom-com remained decidedly straight for much of its existence.

There wasn't a gay rom-com from a major Hollywood movie studio until 2022, when the brash comedy *Bros* was released. But *Bros* also wasn't the first-ever rom-com with an LGBTQ+ couple at its center. While straight couples were falling in love on-screen at multi-plexes, you had to go to an art house to find queer love stories.

Do or *should* queer rom-coms fit into the same format as straight ones? That's a question that many gay rom-coms ask. The answer

OPPOSITE: Winston Chao, May Chin, and Mitchell Lichtenstein in *The Wedding Banquet* (1993).

Michael T. Weiss and Steven Weber on a date in *Jeffrey* (1995), a queer rom-com.

tends to be: yes and no. For as frequently as gay rom-coms subvert the expectations that come along with the genre, the romantic beats don't change. Nor do the meet-cutes.

More rom-coms with LGBTQ+ themes started to emerge in the 1990s and 2000s, around the same time the genre was having its heyday. But while Meg Ryan and Tom Hanks just had to worry about the gentrification of the Upper West Side, there were bigger concerns at play in various corners of the gay community.

Jeffrey (1995) is an exuberant movie with asides to the camera and absurdist scenarios, including Nathan Lane as a gay Catholic priest who starts belting out show tunes after propositioning the eponymous hero. But *Jeffrey*, written by Paul Rudnick, based on his own play and directed by Christopher Ashley, is also a movie about the AIDS crisis. The protagonist, Jeffrey (Steven Weber), decides in the opening moments of the film that he's going to abstain from having sex because he's tired of the fear associated with getting AIDS. But just after making that decision, he meets the attractive Steve (Michael T. Weiss) at the gym. They are immediately attracted to each other, but Jeffrey had made up his mind regarding his celibacy. He starts having doubts about his decision when mutual friends coincidentally set him up with Steve, but then he learns that Steve is HIV-positive and doubles down on his choice to avoid sex.

Jeffrey is often tragic, as any movie about the AIDS crisis should be. During the climax, Jeffrey's dear friend Darius (Bryan Batt), the boyfriend of Sterling (Patrick Stewart), dies. Sterling is inconsolable and angry at Jeffrey for his fear of living. In a vision, Darius appears to Jeffrey—he's wearing a costume from *Cats* because he was a dancer—and tells him: "Hate AIDS, Jeffrey, not life." It's the motivation Jeffrey needs to reach out to Steve and finally embark on a romance.

In an interview in 2021, Rudnick explained that, when the film was initially getting produced, stars were afraid to sign on because of the subject matter, and many only joined once he enlisted Sigourney Weaver, cameoing as a motivational speaker. But as touchy as the subject matter was, Rudnick knew from *Jeffrey*'s theater run that people loved just how romantic it was. And *Jeffrey is* romantic. It ends with a kiss and a shot of a balloon flying up over the New York skyline.

Five years later, Jamie Babbit's 2000 debut feature *But I'm a Cheerleader* faced a more critical reception for not being serious enough in the wake of the AIDS crisis. The pink-saturated satire follows a cheerleader named Megan, played by Natasha Lyonne, who is sent to a conversion camp after her parents suspect that she is gay, even though she's not so sure about her own sexuality. Any feelings of uncertainty, however, clear up when she arrives at the facility and meets a bunch of other queer kids and finds her place. She also comes into contact with the captivating Graham, played by Clea DuVall, who seduces her through little touches and brings her to her first gay bar.

Babbit told the publication *Them* in an interview on the movie's twentieth anniversary: "I wanted to tell a lesbian love story where they don't kill each other at the end or someone dies. I wanted it to have a happy ending, like a fun romantic comedy." Graham at first doesn't want to run away with Megan during the camp's graduation—which involves frilly pink dresses. But then Megan emerges in a cheerleader outfit with a confession of love: "One two three four, you're the one that I adore. Five six seven eight, the one for me 'cause this is fate." Graham runs after her, jumps in the back of the truck, and they drive

Natasha Lyonne and Clea DuVall in gay conversion camp rom-com *But I'm a Cheerleader* (2000).

away kissing. And so, in the face of that backdrop, what surprised Babbit was how initially resistant the larger gay community was to the film. "When the movie got released, I got a lot of really mean reviews, mostly from gay people, because they were so pissed off that I had made a comedy about such a fucked-up subject," she said, noting that tackling the topic of conversion therapy was seen as politically inappropriate. At the same time, star Clea DuVall, who was gay, was terrified of coming out or being outed by her work in the film. She described the press tour as "dangerous." For as radical as *But I'm a Cheerleader* was, it was still emerging at a time when Hollywood was far from accepting of gay actors.

Cheryl Dunye's *The Watermelon Woman* (1997) addresses the industry's systematic exclusion of marginalized people head-on. The groundbreaking movie—the first feature film ever released by a Black lesbian—follows its heroine's romantic escapades as well as her investigation into a lost Black star of old Hollywood known as "The Watermelon Woman." More of a comedy with romantic elements than a rom-com, *The Watermelon Woman* is less focused on giving its heroine a conclusion in the arms of a lover than it is on giving her an emotionally rich journey with her art.

The Watermelon Woman was released in 1997, the same year as another gay-themed rom-com, with a much touchier reputation. Is Kevin Smith's *Chasing Amy* unrepentantly offensive or surprisingly progressive for its time? The movie stars Ben Affleck as a guy who falls for a lesbian (Joey Lauren Adams). In his male bravado, he still pursues her, and she does end up briefly falling for him. It ultimately doesn't work out. It's a film that's still debated and wrestled with by queer audiences. Some have praised its portrayal of bisexuality, while others have voiced frustration with Amy's character. Smith told BuzzFeed in 2017 that it was more a movie about himself than one that was making any sort of broad statement about the lesbian community. "As much as it's a movie that's closely identified with the gay community, by virtue of the fact that the main character was gay, I really never think about it as such," he said. "To me, it was about a boy who grows up to become a man but loses everything in the process—very bittersweet."

Chasing Amy is in a subset of rom-coms about straight people wrestling with their sexuality. This category also includes *Kissing Jessica Stein* (2002), written by and starring Heather Juergensen and Jennifer Westfeldt. Westfeldt plays the title character, a straight woman who answers a personal ad placed by Juergensen's Helen. Jessica ultimately ends up with a man but explores the contours of her own desire.

Two notable gay rom-coms deal with the expectations of traditional parents coming into conflict with a younger generation. Ang Lee's *The Wedding Banquet* (1993) follows a gay couple living in Williamsburg, Brooklyn (before it was as trendy as can be). When Wai-Tung's (Winston Chao) parents say they are coming to visit, his partner, Simon (Mitchell Lichtenstein), encourages him to marry his artist tenant, Wei-Wei (May Chin), both to appease his folks and to help her get her green card. Wai-Tung and Wei-Wei go through all the motions of an extravagant wedding, and their fake relationship turns into genuine affection, which tests Simon and Wai-Tung's love. Fear of Wai-Tung's parents' lack of acceptance almost tears the central couple apart, but it turns out Wai-Tung's parents are far more tolerant of their son's relationship than anyone could have expected. The farce was not for naught, but it was largely unnecessary.

About ten years later, in 2004, Alice Wu made a different film about a child trying to hide herself from her parents in *Saving Face*. Here Eastern conservatism and Western mores come into conflict in a rom-com shell. In the film Wil Pang (Michelle Krusiec) is a young doctor who grudgingly attends dances in Queens' Chinatown to appear as though she's interested in finding a match for the sake of her mother, Hwei-Lan Gao (Joan Chen). But she's not interested

Wil, played by Michelle Krusiec, and Vivian, played by Lynn Chen, dance together in the finale of *Saving Face* (2004).

in any of these dudes: She's a lesbian, and she starts to fall for Vivian (Lynn Chen), a dancer who happens to be her boss's daughter. The situation grows more complicated when it turns out that Wil's mother is pregnant with an unknown man's baby, and, ostracized from her own community, moves in with Wil. As Wil's relationship is developing, she's also trying to keep her mom in the dark about her sexuality, all while her mother is maintaining her own secret.

Wu thinks she got "lucky." She wrote her screenplay when she wasn't yet working in Hollywood. She did so to prove to herself that she could, and, eventually, was able to direct it herself and make it without major alterations. But she also wasn't trying to change the industry. She had a specific purpose in mind. She wanted to make the movie for her mother and her community. "Asian lesbians weren't as visible then," she told me. "There's a deeper sense of: Well, if I'm not going to try, then who's supposed to?"

As an example of just how slow Hollywood is to evolve, it's worth noting that Wu didn't release another film until sixteen years later with *The Half of It* (2020), a teen-centered queer love story with a *Cyrano de Bergerac* bent. And yet, Hollywood is changing. In 2018, 20th Century Fox released *Love, Simon*, based on a young adult novel, about a young man's coming-out journey and his relationship with a mysterious online connection (who happens to attend his high school) who goes by the pseudonym Blue. Rom-com fans flocked to streamers to watch the lesbian holiday romance *Happiest Season*, directed by *But I'm a Cheerleader* star Clea DuVall, in 2020; *Single All the Way* (2021), another LGBTQ+ Christmas rom-com, landed on Netflix the following year. And in 2022 there were not one but two major gay rom-coms to emerge: *Fire Island* on Hulu and *Bros*.

Written by the comedian Joel Kim Booster, *Fire Island* is a revisionist take on *Pride and Prejudice* about a group of gay friends vacationing at the eponymous getaway. Booster's movie explores class and racism in the LGBTQ+ community, as his character Noah starts a tense relationship with seemingly stuck-up lawyer Will (Conrad Ricamora), who stays in the fancier part of town. Will is the Mr. Darcy to Noah's Elizabeth Bennet.

Then, four months after *Fire Island* arrived, *Bros* hit theaters. Almost as soon as it starts, it's clear that *Bros* is a movie that is very conscious about its place in the rom-com ecosystem. It begins with writer and star Billy Eichner's character Bobby Lieber complaining on his podcast about his experience being asked by Hollywood to make a gay rom-com. He dismisses the idea, arguing that straight people aren't actually interested in gay romance, before the movie proceeds to give you a slick gay rom-com that's full of Ephron references, while also being about as sexually explicit as an R-rated movie can get.

Bros was directed by rom-com veteran (and straight man) Nicholas Stoller, of *Forgetting Sarah Marshall* (2008) fame, but was almost as inclusive as possible, even with two cisgender men as its leads. Nearly every character in the film is played by a queer person, even nonqueer roles. *Bros* took its burden of representation seriously. But when *Bros* came out, it's not as if the rom-com, in the words of Cary Grant, went gay "all of a sudden." It was probably a little gay all along, and as time goes on it will only get more so.

ROLL CREDITS

The pleasure of discovering a good rom-com—whether new or old—is ineffable. Throughout the course of researching this book, I revisited myriad old favorites—the films that had shaped my affection for this genre. I returned to the likes of *The Philadelphia Story* and *You've Got Mail.* I found my most treasured moments in *Sabrina* and *It Happened One Night.* I watched *Moonstruck* at the Paris Theater in New York after introducing it to a packed house. When the event was over, I was approached by a couple from out of town. They had been watching every Nicolas Cage movie and had been trying to cue up *Moonstruck* the night before in their hotel room. They walked by the marquee and saw it was playing and came inside. It was fate. It was like something out of a rom-com.

But I've also been discovering classic films I had never encountered before—like *A Foreign Affair* or *Claudine*—which have now become part of my personal canon. And sometimes, just sometimes, I'll come across an entirely new romantic comedy that captures my heart. For instance, in early 2023 I was preparing for the Sundance Film Festival when I watched *Rye Lane*, a British rom-com about a chance encounter that turns into a wild day and, ultimately, a love story.

Because, yes, though it's had its ups and downs, the rom-com is still thriving, despite what some of the naysayers might have you

OPPOSITE: Constance Wu and Henry Golding help keep the rom-com alive with *Crazy Rich Asians* (2018).

believe. For decades, fans have been either mourning the death of the rom-com or celebrating its revival. So which is it? (Neither.) And can you ever really kill the rom-com? (No.)

When did all this anxiety over the state of the rom-com start? In 2013 the *Hollywood Reporter* published a not-quite obituary for the genre. Producer Joy Gorman told the trade publication that "the meet-cute is dead," and the writer, Tatiana Siegel, argued that "As studios increasingly focus on films that can be sequelized and play in overseas markets, the one-off, dialogue-dependent rom-coms are a difficult sell. In addition, the decreasing appeal of young movie stars is translating into less demand for romantic pairings built around their star power." In 2016 Emily Yahr in the *Washington Post* authored an oft-cited essay arguing, "The rom-com is dead. Good."

But none of this is new, as Jen Chaney wrote in a 2017 piece in *New York* magazine, titled "The Romantic Comedy Is Not Dead—It's Just Not the Same As You Remember." Chaney begins her story by citing a 1992 article by Peter Rainer in the *Los Angeles Times* that states, "We're used to thinking of certain genres, despite an occasional flare-up, as being essentially dead—the musical, for example, or the western. It doesn't seem possible that something as basic as the romantic comedy could join their company, and yet that's what seems to be happening. And it's happening when it could be a golden time for romantic comedy. Certainly, there have never been as many wildly talented and funny actresses around." At that point Rainer's problem wasn't that studios didn't want to make rom-coms; it was that the rom-coms weren't what they used to be.

So as you can see, we're going in circles here.

And it's true. In the 2020s, Hollywood isn't keen on making movies at the kind of mid-budget that rom-coms fall into, often opting for superhero or franchise fare. And it's also true that for a while it didn't seem like stars were all that interested in attaching themselves to rom-coms, though the tide is turning there as well.

For every time someone wants to say the rom-com is dead, the rom-com seems to rear its head again. When *Crazy Rich Asians* came out in 2018 and was a massive hit—making over $170 million in the United States—it was seen as a win for both Asian representation and the rom-com. Audiences would still turn out for a flashy romantic extravaganza. In 2022, there were three major studio rom-coms with big movie stars: *The Lost City* with Sandra Bullock, *Ticket to Paradise* with Julia Roberts and George Clooney, and *Marry Me* with Jennifer Lopez. In late 2023, *Anyone But You*, a riff on *Much Ado About Nothing* starring Sydney Sweeney and Glen Powell, defied box office expectations to make over $216 million worldwide, proving that rom-coms with up-and-coming talent can succeed. At the same time, there are exciting innovations in smaller arenas, like *Rye Lane*.

But if you've read this far, you know that the rom-com is always changing and is never quite as simple as its 1990s reputation would make it out to be. There are formulas to it, yes, but there are also constant subversions of those formulas.

The rom-com will never fully go away because romance will never really go away. And romance is messy and funny and makes for great movies. Plenty have tried to write off rom-coms as being contrived or insubstantial, but to do so ignores what the rom-com tells us about social customs from the Depression to the present day. The negotiations of love are as important to us now as they were to Preston Sturges's or Billy Wilder's heroes and heroines; the mechanisms have just shifted. Longing is an essential tradition; rom-coms just happen to add jokes. And that's why we love them so.

Albee, George Sumner. Letter to Billy Wilder, September 1, 1960. Billy Wilder Papers. Margaret Herrick Library, Academy Museum of Motion Pictures.

B., Brian. "Director James L. Brooks Talks Spanglish." MovieWeb. December 16, 2004. https://movieweb.com/director-james-l-brooks-talks-spanglish/.

BBC News. "Obituary: Doris Day, America's Archetypal Girl Next Door." May 13, 2019. https://www.bbc.com/news/entertainment-arts-13202284.

Bennetts, Leslie. "In Kate Country." *Vanity Fair.* October 2000. https://archive.vanityfair.com/article/2000/10/in-kate-country.

Bergeson, Samantha. "Clea DuVall: Promoting 'But I'm a Cheerleader' Was 'Dangerous' while in the Closet." IndieWire. October 17, 2022. https://www.indiewire.com/2022/10/clea-duvall-but-im-a-cheerleader-scary-time-1234773201/.

Bernstein, Adam. "Doris Day, Singer and Perpetually Chaste Movie Star of the 1950s and '60s, Dies at 97." *Washington Post.* May 13, 2019. https://www.washingtonpost.com/local/obituaries/doris-day-singer-and-perpetually-chaste-movie-star-of-the-1950s-and-60s-dies-at-97/2019/05/13/c86cb9ae-757f-11e9-bd25-c989555e7766_story.html.

Bianco, Marcie, and Merryn Johns. "The Most Daring Thing about Katharine Hepburn? Her Pants." *Vanity Fair.* May 12, 2016. https://www.vanityfair.com/hollywood/2016/05/katharine-hepburn-style-pants.

Blowen, Michael. "Jean Arthur at 80: A Legend Made of Style and Substance, not Publicity." *Chicago Tribune.* October 20, 1985. https://www.chicagotribune.com/news/ct-xpm-1985-10-20-8503110672-story.html.

Bond, Mindy. "Michael Showalter, Comedian & Filmmaker." Gothamist. June 10, 2005. https://gothamist.com/arts-entertainment/michael-showalter-comedian-filmmaker.

"Cameron on Wilder: Various Quotes." The Uncool. Accessed May 7, 2023. https://www.theuncool.com/books/conversations-with-wilder/cameron-on-wilder-various-quotes/.

Canby, Vincent. "Reviews/Film; A Terminal Ad Man, a God, and a South Pacific Volcano." *New York Times.* March 9, 1990. https://www.nytimes.com/1990/03/09/movies/reviews-film-a-terminal-ad-man-a-god-and-a-south-pacific-volcano.html.

Canfield, Alyce. "Are You the Girl for Cary Grant?" *Movieland.* March 1947.

"Cary Grant: $250,000 a Picture?" *Screenland*. February 1938.

Cavell, Stanley. *Pursuits of Happiness: The Hollywood Comedy of Remarriage.* Cambridge, MA: Harvard University Press, 1984.

Chaney, Jen. "The Romantic Comedy Is Not Dead—It's Just Not the Same as You Remember." Vulture. January 30, 2017. https://www.vulture.com/2017/01 /romantic-comedy-is-not-dead.html.

Crowe, Cameron. "Conversations with Billy." *Vanity Fair.* October 7, 1999. https:// www.vanityfair.com/news/1999/10/billy-wilder-199910.

Crowe, Cameron. *Conversations with Wilder.* New York: Knopf, 1999.

Crowther, Bosley. "Against a Sea of Troubles; In 'To Be or Not to Be,' Ernst Lubitsch Has Opposed Real Tragedy with an Incongruous Comedy Plot— Other New Films." *New York Times*. March 22, 1942. https://www.nytimes .com/1942/03/22/archives/against-a-sea-of-troubles-in-to-be-or-not-to-be -ernst-lubitsch-has.html.

———. "Jean Arthur, Marlene Dietrich and John Land a Triangle in 'A Foreign Affair.'" *New York Times*. July 1, 1948. https://www.nytimes .com/1948/07/01/archives/jean-arthur-marlene-dietrich-and-john-land-a -triangle-in-a-foreign.html.

———. "'More the Merrier,' Sparkling Comedy, Opens at Music Hall—'Lady of Bur-lesque'; with Barbara Stanwyck, at Capitol." *New York Times*. May 14, 1943. https://www.nytimes.com/1943/05/14/archives/more-the-merrier-sparkling -comedy-opens-at-music-hall-lady-of.html.

———. "The Screen; 'I Married a Witch,' a Thorne Smith Whimsey, with Fredric March and Veronica Lake as Stars, Arrives at the Capitol." *New York Times*. November 20, 1942. https://www.nytimes.com/1942/11/20/archives/the -screen-i-married-a-witch-a-thorne-smith-whimsey-with-fredric.html.

———. "Screwball Comedy; 'My Man Godfrey' Dips into an Old Film Style." *New York Times*. October 20, 1957. https://www.nytimes.com/1957/10/20 /archives/screwball-comedy-my-man-godfrey-dips-into-an-old-film-style.html.

———. "'Woman of Year,' with Katharine Hepburn and Spencer Tracy, at Music Hall—'Design for Scandal' Opens at Capitol." *New York Times*. February 6, 1942. https://www.nytimes.com/1942/02/06/archives/woman-of-year-with -katharine-hepburn-and-spencer-tracy-at-music.html.

Cuby, Michael. "Jamie Babbit Always Knew 'But I'm a Cheerleader' Was Ahead of Its Time." Them. December 8, 2020. https://www.them.us/story /but-im-a-cheerleader-20th-anniversary-jaime-babbit-interview.

BIBLIOGRAPHY

Deere, Dorothy. "Charles Coburn Is Really a Character." *Movieland*. June 1944. https://archive.org/details/movielandtvtimev02unse/page/n907/mode/2up?view=theater.

Dowd, Maureen. "Opinion: Can You Eat in Bed?" *New York Times*. August 1, 2009. https://www.nytimes.com/2009/08/02/opinion/02dowd.html.

Ebert, Roger. Review of *The Heartbreak Kid*, directed by Elaine May. RogerEbert.com. January 1, 1972. https://www.rogerebert.com/reviews/the-heartbreak-kid-1972.

Edwards, Anne. *Katharine Hepburn: A Remarkable Woman*. New York: St. Martin's Press, 2000.

"Elaine May in Conversation with Mike Nichols." *Film Comment*. July/August 2006. https://www.filmcomment.com/article/elaine-may-in-conversation-with-mike-nichols/.

Ephron, Nora. "Nora Ephron: Flops, I've Had a Few." *The Guardian*. February 10, 2011. https://www.theguardian.com/film/2011/feb/10/nora-ephron-i-remember-nothing.

———. "Nora Ephron's Favorite Love Stories." Daily Beast. February 14, 2012. https://www.thedailybeast.com/articles/2010/02/11/nora-ephrons-top-11-romantic-comedies.

Erbland, Kate. "The True Story of *Pretty Woman*'s Original Dark Ending." *Vanity Fair*. March 23, 2015. https://www.vanityfair.com/hollywood/2015/03/pretty-woman-original-ending.

Eyman, Scott. *Ernst Lubitsch: Laughter in Paradise*. New York: Simon & Schuster, 1993.

Farber, Stephen. "Film; Hugh Grant Makes Them Think of Cary Grant." *New York Times*. February 27, 1994. https://www.nytimes.com/1994/02/27/movies/film-hugh-grant-makes-them-think-of-cary-grant.html.

Garber, Megan. "The Quiet Cruelty of 'When Harry Met Sally.'" *The Atlantic*. July 19, 2019. https://www.theatlantic.com/entertainment/archive/2019/07/when-harry-met-sally-and-the-high-maintenance-woman/594382/.

Goldstein, Patrick. "How One Actor Changed a Movie Before It Even Came Out." *Los Angeles Times*. June 23, 1997. https://www.latimes.com/archives/la-xpm-1997-06-23-ca-6094-story.html.

Handler, Rachel. "John Patrick Shanley on His Trio of Unhinged Rom-Coms." Vulture. December 22, 2020. https://www.vulture.com/2020/12/john-patrick-shanley-on-his-trio-of-unhinged-rom-coms.html.

Haring, Bruce. "Director Nancy Meyers Channels Ernst Lubitsch, Confirms Origin of 'Paris Paramount' Film Title." Deadline. March 19, 2023. https://deadline.com/2023/03/director-nancy-meyers-channels-ernst-lubitsch-confirms-origin-paris-paramount-film-title-1235304139/.

Harmetz, Aljean. "Barbara Stanwyck: 'I'm a Tomorrow Woman.'" *New York Times*. March 22, 1981. https://www.nytimes.com/1981/03/22/arts/barbara-stanwyck-m-tomorrow-woman-los-angeles-it-was-after-third-fourth-letter.html.

Hopper, Hedda. "British Press Lauds Doris Day's Comedy." *Los Angeles Times*. June 2, 1959.

Hunter, Stephen. "'Addicted to Love': Hell Hath No Fury, Like Meg Ryan." *Washington Post*. May 23, 1997. https://www.washingtonpost.com/wp-srv/style/longterm/movies/videos/addictedtolovehunter.htm.

Ifeanyi, K. C. "'Yesterday,' 'Love Actually' Screenwriter Richard Curtis Breaks Down His Most Iconic Rom-Coms." Fast Company. June 28, 2019. https://www.fastcompany.com/90370484/screenwriting-legend-richard-curtis-breaks-down-his-most-iconic-rom-coms.

Itzkoff, Dave. "Dalton Trumbo's Screenwriting Credit Restored to 'Roman Holiday.'" ArtsBeat. December 20, 2011. https://archive.nytimes.com/artsbeat.blogs.nytimes.com/2011/12/20/dalton-trumbos-screenwriting-credit-restored-to-roman-holiday/.

James, Caryn. "Review/Film; It's Harry [Loves] Sally in a Romance of New Yorkers and Neuroses." *New York Times*. July 12, 1989. https://www.nytimes.com/1989/07/12/movies/review-film-it-s-harry-loves-sally-in-a-romance-of-new-yorkers-and-neuroses.html.

Jamison, Jack. "Cary versus Gary." *Photoplay*. January 1933.

Jones, Kent. "Interview: Woody Allen." *Film Comment*. May/June 2011. https://www.filmcomment.com/article/woody-allen-the-film-comment-interview/.

Kaiser, Vrai. "Society's Bisexual Hangups: How 'Chasing Amy' Is Still Ahead of Its Time." The Mary Sue. August 2, 2015. https://www.themarysue.com/chasing-amy-still-ahead-of-its-time/.

Kaplan, Ilana. "'To All the Boys I've Loved Before' . . . and to Fans Hungry for More." *New York Times*. February 12, 2020. https://www.nytimes.com/2020/02/12/movies/to-all-the-boys-ps-i-still-love-you.html.

"Katie Gets Her Man." *Screenland*. January 1950. https://lantern.mediahist.org/catalog/screenland54unse_0183.

Kaufman, Amy. "Drew Barrymore Is Too Much—and That's Just Right." *Los Angeles Times*. March 5, 2023. https://www.latimes.com/entertainment-arts /story/2023-03-05/for-real-drew-barrymore-talk-show.

Keating, Shannon. "Looking Back at the Sexual Politics of 'Chasing Amy' 20 Years Later." BuzzFeed News. April 18, 2017. https://www.buzzfeednews .com/article/shannonkeating/chasing-amy-20-years-later.

Kempley, Rita. "A Little Sex, Please, He's British." *Washington Post*. March 20, 1994. https://www.washingtonpost.com/archive/lifestyle/style/1994/03/20 /a-little-sex-please-hes-british/4c4af3de-0428-4436-9a60-a2e2eb0ecb83/.

Kinane, Ruth. "'My Best Friend's Wedding' Director Explains Flawed Original Ending." *Entertainment Weekly*. March 31, 2017. https://ew.com /movies/2017/03/31/my-best-friends-wedding-alternate-ending/.

Kiriakou, Olympia. "Notebook Primer: Screwball Comedy." MUBI. January 6, 2022. https://mubi.com/notebook/posts/notebook-primer-screwball-comedy.

Lang, Cady. "20 of the Sweetest, Funniest, and Most Outrageous Meet-Cutes in Rom-Com History."*Time*. September 23, 2022. https://time.com/6215146 /best-rom-coms-meet-cutes/.

Lang, Kevin. "The Big Sick (2017)." History vs Hollywood. June 20, 2017. https:// www.historyvshollywood.com/reelfaces/the-big-sick/.

Luscombe, Belinda. "Rom-Com Master Richard Curtis Is Still Trying to Prove That All We Need Is Love." *Time*. June 20, 2019. https://time.com/5610727 /richard-curtis-yesterday-movie-interview/.

Marchese, David. "Meg Ryan on Romantic Comedies, Celebrity and Leaving It All Behind." *New York Times*. February 15, 2019. https://www.nytimes.com /interactive/2019/02/15/magazine/meg-ryan-romantic-comedy.html.

Maslin, Janet. "Film Review; The Blossoming of a Wallflower." *New York Times*. April 21, 1995. https://www.nytimes.com/1995/04/21/movies/film-review -the-blossoming-of-a-wallflower.html.

McConaughey, Matthew. *Greenlights*. New York: Crown, 2020.

McGrath, Charles. "Mike Nichols, Master of Invisibility." *New York Times*. April 10, 2009. https://www.nytimes.com/2009/04/12/movies/12mcgr.html.

Mernit, Billy. *Writing the Romantic Comedy: The Art of Crafting Funny Love Stories for the Screen*. New York: Harper, 2020.

Meroney, John, and Patricia Beauchamp. "James L. Brooks on Journalism, the Oscars, and 'Broadcast News.'" *The Atlantic*. February 26, 2011. https:// www.theatlantic.com/entertainment/archive/2011/02/james-l-brooks-on -journalism-the-oscars-and-broadcast-news/71744/.

BIBLIOGRAPHY

Meslow, Scott. "'Nora Ephron Interviewed Me Like a Journalist': Billy Crystal and Rob Reiner on Making When Harry Met Sally." inews.co.uk. February 14, 2022, https://inews.co.uk/culture/film/billy-crystal-rob-reiner-when-harry-met-sally-nora-ephron-romcom-history-1458448.

Mooney, Joshua. "Adam and Drew: Sandler and Barrymore Enjoy Bubbly Chemistry in 'The Wedding Singer.'" *The Times* (Munster, Indiana). February 13, 1998.

Morgan, Kim. "Jean Arthur, the Nonconformist." The Criterion Collection. May 4, 2020. https://www.criterion.com/current/posts/6930-jean-arthur-the-nonconformist.

Morris, Hal. "Teen-Agers Keep Films Above Water." *Los Angeles Mirror.* May 18, 1959.

Murphy, Mary Jo. "The Pokemon Go of the 1930s: Excuse Me, I Need to Find a Monkey and Head to the Waldorf." *New York Times.* July 21, 2016. https://www.nytimes.com/2016/07/22/arts/excuse-me-i-need-to-find-a-monkey-and-head-to-the-waldorf-asap.html.

Nelson, E. S. "The All-American Favorites of 1962." *Box Office.* April 15, 1963. https://lantern.mediahist.org/catalog/boxofficebarometer 1963-04-15-62-63_0018.

Nugent, Frank S. "The Screen; 'My Man Godfrey.'" *New York Times.* September 18, 1936. https://www.nytimes.com/1936/09/18/archives/the-screen-my-man-godfrey.html.

Pasquini, Maria, and Liz McNeil. "Inside Doris Day's Long-Lasting Friendship with Rock Hudson and Final Goodbye." *People.* May 13, 2019. https://people.com/movies/doris-day-enduring-friendship-rock-hudson/.

"Interviews: Drew Barrymore on 50 First Dates." ComingSoon.Net. January 28, 2004. https://www.comingsoon.net/extras/features/3188-interviews-drew-barrymore-on-50-first-dates.

Persall, Steve. "Big Ideas on Relationships." *Tampa Bay Times.* June 20, 1993.

Petersen, Anne Helen. "Jennifer Lawrence and the History of Cool Girls." BuzzFeed. February 28, 2014. https://www.buzzfeed.com/annehelenpetersen/jennifer-lawrence-and-the-history-of-cool-girls.

Phipps, Keith. "The Darker Side of Tom Hanks." The Ringer. November 19, 2019. https://www.theringer.com/movies/2019/11/19/20970642/tom-hanks-darker-roles-mr-rogers.

Rainer, Peter. "Film Comment: Why Do the Movies Kiss Off Romance?" *Los Angeles Times.* October 11, 1992. https://www.latimes.com/archives/la-xpm-1992-10-11-ca-498-story.html.

"The Reviewers Box." *Movieland.* January 1950. https://archive.org/details/movielandtvtimev07unse/page/94/mode/2up?view=theater.

Roettgers, Janko. "More Than 80 Million Subscribers Watched Netflix Rom-Coms This Summer." *Variety.* October 16, 2018. https://variety.com/2018/digital/news/netflix-rom-coms-80-million-1202981966/.

Rosenfeld, Megan. "'Government Girls': World War II's Army of the Potomac." *Washington Post.* May 10, 1999. https://www.washingtonpost.com/wp-srv/local/2000/govgirls0510.htm.

Sanchez, Charles. "Pretty, Witty, and Gay: Revisiting HIV Classic 'Jeffrey' with Paul Rudnick." TheBody. July 12, 2021. https://www.thebody.com/article/paul-rudnick-jeffrey-hiv-aids-play-film.

Schallert, Edwin. "Sex Apple Just 'Hooey'—Claudette Colbert." *Los Angeles Times.* March 4, 1934.

Schlosser, Kurt. "Dustin Hoffman's Tearful 'Tootsie' Interview about Women Goes Viral." Today.com. July 9, 2013. http://www.today.com/popculture/dustin-hoffmans-tearful-tootsie-interview-about-women-goes-viral-6C10578440.

Scott, A. O. "Doris Day: A Hip Sex Goddess Disguised as the Girl Next Door." *New York Times.* May 14, 2019. https://www.nytimes.com/2019/05/14/movies/doris-day-appreciation.html.

Seymore, Hart. "Carole Lombard Tells: 'How I Live by a Man's Code.'" *Photoplay.* September 1937. Quoted on The Screwball Girl, December 15, 2020. https://thescrewballgirl.com/articles/1930s/carole-lombard-tells-how-i-live-by-a-mans-code-photoplay-september-1937/.

Siegel, Tatiana. "R.I.P. Romantic Comedies: Why Harry Wouldn't Meet Sally in 2013." *The Hollywood Reporter.* September 26, 2013. https://www.hollywoodreporter.com/news/general-news/rip-romantic-comedies-why-harry-634776/.

Sikov, Ed. *Screwball: Hollywood's Madcap Romantic Comedies.* New York: Crown Publishers, 1989.

Smith, Jack. "Come Gaze into My Attitude Profile." *San Francisco Examiner.* March 6, 1983.

———. "Jack Smith." *Los Angeles Times.* April 3, 1983.

"'Stanwyck': Fan Fare with Glossy Gossip." *Washington Post.* Accessed February 4, 2023. https://www.washingtonpost.com/archive/lifestyle/1984/03/27/stanwyck-fan-fare-with-glossy-gossip/9f93f72a-591c-4b0a-91fc-6b0062a35945/.

Strause, Jackie. "How 'My Big Fat Greek Wedding' Became an Indie Phenomenon." *Hollywood Reporter.* March 25, 2016. https://www.hollywoodreporter.com/news/general-news/how-my-big-fat-greek-878417/.

Sturges, Preston, and Sandy Sturges. *Preston Sturges.* New York: Simon and Schuster, 1990.

Surmelian, Leon. "Public Bachelor No. 1 (Cary Grant)." *Motion Picture.* February 1938.

Svetkey, Benjamin. "From the EW Archives: Tom Hanks and Meg Ryan Reunite for 'You've Got Mail.'" *Entertainment Weekly.* December 18, 1998.

Syme, Rachel. "The Nora Ephron We Forget." *New Yorker.* August 15, 2022. https://www.newyorker.com/magazine/2022/08/22/the-nora-ephron-we-forget.

Warner, Kara. "James L. Brooks Reveals 'Broadcast News' Deleted Subplot and 'Fascinating' Alternate Ending." MTV.com. December 15, 2010. https://www.mtv.com/news/yoz704/james-l-brooks-broadcast-news-deleted-subplot-alternate-ending.

Wolcott, James. "Lovers Come Back." *Vanity Fair.* April 2000. https://archive.vanityfair.com/article/share/31f786c9-8870-410b-97c4-4b1754220426?itm_content=footer-recirc.

———. "Ryan's Laughter." *Vanity Fair.* December 1989. https://archive.vanityfair.com/article/1989/12/ryans-laughter.

Yahr, Emily. "The Rom-Com Is Dead. Good." *Washington Post.* October 8, 2016. https://www.washingtonpost.com/lifestyle/style/the-rom-com-is-dead-good/2016/10/06/6d82a934-859c-11e6-ac72-a29979381495_story.html.

Zeman, Ned. "Canoodling with Julia." *Vanity Fair.* June 1999. https://archive.vanityfair.com/article/1999/6/canoodling-with-julia.

The meet-cute that generated this book started with Shannon Fabricant, first in college and then as my editor for my two previous Running Press books. She brought on the wonderful Maria Riillo to shepherd this project with the help of Turner Classic Movies.

Thank you to the Margaret Herrick Library for letting me spend time in your collection.

While I don't consider myself a rom-com queen, I do have some great friends who were the Maries to my Sally, and were always there for support and guidance. They also allowed me to panic and complain in the context of writing this book, and for that I am so grateful to Lindsay, David, Hillary, Alison, and so many more.

Mom and Dad, thank you for taking me to see *You've Got Mail* when I was eight years old and loading me up on all of the classics. Thanks for buying that Preston Sturges box set. I wouldn't be on this planet if it weren't for you, but I also wouldn't love rom-coms as much as I do if you hadn't planted that seed.

Cathy, thank you for coaching me in the vintage style of Audrey Hepburn.

Bob: You had me at hello when you swiped on Bumble. Just kidding, it took a while for me to respond. That said, now you are my Harry Burns, my best friend and my true love, and I'm so glad I get to do this by your side. Also, we've raised an adorable dog child, Daisy. I love you.